INSTINCTS OF THE HERD IN PEACE AND WAR

INSTINCTS OF THE HERD IN PEACE AND WAR

WILFRED TROTTER

COSIMO CLASSICS

NEW YORK

Instincts of the Herd in Peace and War

© 2005 Cosimo, Inc.

All rights reserved. No part of this book may be used or
reproduced in any manner whatsoever without prior written
permission except in the case of brief quotations embodied in
critical articles or reviews. For information, address:
Cosimo, P.O. Box 416, Old Chelsea Station,
New York, NY 10113-0416

or visit our website at:
www.cosimobooks.com

Instincts of the Herd in Peace and War originally published by
T. Fisher Unwin Ltd. in 1916.

Library of Congress Cataloging-in-Publication Data
A catalog record for this book is available
from the Library of Congress

Cover design by www.wiselephant.com

ISBN: 1-59605-076-4

PREFACE

THE first two essays in this book were written some ten years ago and published in the *Sociological Review* in 1908 and 1909. They had formed a single paper, but it was found necessary to publish in two instalments at an interval of six months, and to cut down to a considerable extent the total bulk.

It was lately suggested to me that as the numbers of the review in which the two essays appeared were out of print, the fact that the subject concerned was not without some current interest might justify a republication. It was not possible to do this without trying to embody such fruits as there might be of ten years' further speculation and some attempt to apply to present affairs the principles which had been sketched out.

The new comment very soon surpassed by far in bulk the original text, and constitutes, in fact, all but a comparatively few pages of this book. This rather minute record is made here not because it has any interest of its own, but especially to point out that I have been engaged in trying to apply to the affairs of to-day principles which had taken shape ten years ago. I point this out not in order

to claim any gift of foresight in having suggested
so long ago reasons for regarding the stability of
civilization as unsuspectedly slight, but because it
is notorious that the atmosphere of a great war
is unfavourable to free speculation. If the principles
upon which my argument is based had been
evolved during the present times, the reader would
have had special reason to suspect their validity,
however plausible they might seem in the refracting
air of national emergency.

The general purpose of this book is to suggest
that the science of psychology is not the mass of
dreary and indefinite generalities of which it sometimes perhaps seems to be made up ; to suggest that,
especially when studied in relation to other branches
of biology, it is capable of becoming a guide in
the actual affairs of life and of giving an understanding of the human mind such as may enable
us in a practical and useful way to foretell some
of the course of human behaviour. The present
state of public affairs gives an excellent chance
for testing the truth of this suggestion, and adds
to the interest of the experiment the strong incentive
of an urgent national peril.

If this war is becoming, as it obviously is, daily
more and more completely a contest of moral forces,
some really deep understanding of the nature and
sources of national morale must be at least as
important a source of strength as the technical
knowledge of the military engineer and the maker
of cannon. One is apt to suppose that the chief
function of a sound morale is the maintenance of

a high courage and resolution through the ups and downs of warfare. In a nation whose actual independence and existence are threatened from without such qualities may be taken for granted and may be present when the general moral forces are seriously disordered. A satisfactory morale gives something much more difficult to attain. It gives smoothness of working, energy and enterprise to the whole national machine, while from the individual it ensures the maximal outflow of effort with a minimal interference from such egoistic passions as anxiety, impatience, and discontent. A practical psychology would define these functions and indicate means by which they are to be called into activity.

The more we consider the conduct of government in warfare the clearer does it become that every act of authority produces effects in two distinct fields—that of its primary function as directed more or less immediately against the enemy, and that of its secondary action upon the morale of the nation. The first of these two constituents possesses the uncertainty of all military enterprises, and its success or failure cannot be foretold ; the influence of the second constituent is susceptible of definition and foresight and need never be wholly ambiguous to any but the ignorant or the indifferent.

The relative importance of the military and the moral factors in any act or enterprise varies much, but it may be asserted that while the moral factor may sometimes be enormously the more important, it is never wholly absent. This constant and admittedly significant factor in all acts of government is usually awarded an attention so thoroughly inexpert and perfunctory as to justify the feeling that the customary belief in its importance is no more than a conventional expression.

The method I have used is frankly speculative, and I make no apology for it because the facts are open to the observation of all and available for confirmation or disproof. I have tried to point out a way ; I have tried not to exhort or persuade to the use of it—these are matters outside my province.

November, 1915.

PREFACE TO THE SECOND EDITION

A few errors in the text of the First Edition have been corrected, and a sentence which had caused misunderstanding has been omitted. No other change has been made. A Postscript has been added in order to point out some of the directions in which the psychological inquiry made during the war gave a practical foresight that was confirmed by the course of events, and in order to examine the remarkable situation in which society now finds itself.

In the Preface to the First Edition I ventured to suggest that some effective knowledge of the mind might be of value to a nation at war ; I take this opportunity of suggesting that such knowledge might be not less useful to a tired nation seeking peace. At the same time it should perhaps be added that this book is concerned wholly with the examination of principles, is professedly speculative in methods and conclusions, and is quite without pretensions to advise upon the conduct of affairs.

August, 1919.

CONTENTS

CONTENTS

INSTINCTS OF THE HERD IN PEACE AND WAR

HERD INSTINCT AND ITS BEARING ON THE PSYCHOLOGY OF CIVILIZED MAN

I. INTRODUCTION

FEW subjects have led to discussion so animated and prolonged as has the definition of the science of sociology. It is therefore necessary, as it is hoped that this essay may be capable of sociological applications, that the writer should define the sense in which he uses the term. By calling it a science is, of course, denoted the view that sociology is a body of knowledge derived from experience of its material and co-ordinated so that it shall be useful in forecasting and, if possible, directing the future behaviour of that material. This material is man in society or associated man.

Sociology, therefore, is obviously but another name for psychology in the widest sense, for, that is to say, a psychology which can include all the phenomena of the mind without the exception even of the most complex, and is essentially practical in a fuller sense than any orthodox psychology which has yet appeared.

Sociology has, of course, often been described as social psychology and has been regarded as differing from ordinary psychology in being concerned with those forms of mental activity which man displays in his social relations, the assumption being made that society brings to light a special series of mental aptitudes with which ordinary psychology, dealing as it does essentially with the individual, is not mainly concerned. It may be stated at once that it is a principal thesis of this essay that this attitude is a fallacious one, and has been responsible for the comparative sterility of the psychological method in sociology. The two fields— the social and the individual—are regarded here as absolutely continuous ; all human psychology, it is contended, must be the psychology of associated man, since man as a solitary animal is unknown to us, and every individual must present the characteristic reactions of the social animal if such exist. The only difference between the two branches of the science lies in the fact that ordinary psychology makes no claim to be practical in the sense of conferring useful foresight ; whereas sociology does profess to deal with the complex, unsimplified problems of ordinary life, ordinary life being, by a biological necessity, social life. If, therefore, sociology is to be defined as psychology, it would be better to call it practical or applied psychology than social psychology.

The first effect of the complete acceptance of this point of view is to render very obvious the difficulty and immensity of the task of sociology ; indeed, the possibility of such a science is sometimes denied. For example, at an early meeting of the Sociological Society, Professor Karl Pearson expressed the opinion that the birth of the science of sociology must await the obstetrical genius of some one man of the calibre of Darwin or Pasteur. At a later meeting Mr. H. G. Wells went farther, and maintained that as a science sociology not only does not but cannot exist.

Such scepticism appears in general to be based upon the idea that a practical psychology in the sense already defined is impossible. According to some this is because the human will introduces into conduct an element necessarily incommensurable, which will always render the behaviour of man subject to the occurrence of true variety and therefore beyond the reach of scientific generalization ; according to another and a more deterministic school, human conduct, while not theoretically liable to true variety in the philosophic sense or to the intrusion of the will as a first cause, is in fact so complex that no reduction of it to a complete system of generalizations will be possible until science in general has made very great progress beyond its present position. Both views lead in practice to attitudes of equal pessimism towards sociology.

The observable complexity of human conduct is, undoubtedly, very great and discouraging. The problem of generalizing from it presents, however, one important peculiarity which is not very evident at first sight. It is that as observers we are constantly pursued by man's own account of his behaviour ; that of a given act our observation is always more or less mixed with a knowledge, derived from our own feelings, of how it seems to the author of the act, and it is much more difficult than is often supposed to disentangle and allow for the influence of this factor. Each of us has the strongest conviction that his conduct and beliefs are fundamentally individual and reasonable and in essence independent of external causation, and each is ready to furnish a series of explanations of his conduct consistent with these principles. These explanations, moreover, are the ones which will occur spontaneously to the observer watching the conduct of his fellows.

It is suggested here that the sense of the unimaginable complexity and variability of human affairs is derived less than is generally supposed from direct observation and more from this second factor of introspectual interpretation which may be called a kind of anthropomorphism. A reaction against this in human psychology is no less necessary therefore than was in comparative psychology the similar movements the extremer developments of which are associated with the names of Bethe, Beer, Uexküll and Nuel. It is contended that it is this anthropomorphism in the general attitude of psychologists which, by disguising the observable uniformities of human conduct, has rendered so slow the establishment of a really practical psychology. Little as the subject has been studied from the point of view of a thorough-going objectivism, yet even now certain generalizations summarising some of the ranges of human belief and conduct might already be formulated. Such an inquiry, however, is not the purpose of this essay, and these considerations have been advanced, in the first place, to suggest that theory indicates that the problem of sociology is not so hopelessly difficult as it at first appears, and secondly, as a justification for an examination of certain aspects of human conduct by the deductive method. The writer would contend that while that method is admittedly dangerous when used as a substitute for a kind of investigation in which deductive processes are reduced to a minimum, yet it has its special field of usefulness in cases where the significance of previously accumulated facts has been misinterpreted, or where the exacter methods have proved unavailing through the investigator having been without indications of precisely what facts were likely to be the most fruitful subject for measurement. This essay, then, will be an attempt to obtain by a deductive consideration of conduct some guidance for the application of those methods of measurement and co-ordination of facts upon which all true science is based.

A very little consideration of the problem of conduct makes it plain that it is in the region of feeling, using the term in its broadest sense, that the key is to be sought. Feeling has relations to instinct as obvious and fundamental as are the analogies between intellectual processes and reflex action; it is with the consideration of instinct, therefore, that this paper must now be occupied.

II. PSYCHOLOGICAL ASPECTS OF INSTINCT.

Many years ago, in a famous chapter of his Text Book of Psychology, William James analysed and established with a quite final delicacy and precision the way in which instinct appears to introspection. He showed that the impulse of an instinct reveals itself as an axiomatically obvious proposition, as something which is so clearly " sense " that any idea of discussing its basis is foolish or wicked.[1]

When we recognize that decisions due to instinct come into the mind in a form so characteristic and easily identifiable we are encouraged at once to ask

[1] Not one man in a billion, when taking his dinner, ever thinks of utility. He eats because the food tastes good and makes him want more. If you ask him why he should want to eat more of what tastes like that, instead of revering you as a philosopher he will probably laugh at you for a fool. The connexion between the savoury sensation and the act it awakens is for him absolute and *selbstverständlich*, an " *a priori* synthesis " of the most perfect sort needing no proof but its own evidence. . . . To the metaphysician alone can such questions occur as : Why do we smile, when pleased, and not scowl ? Why are we unable to talk to a crowd as to a single friend ? Why does a particular maiden turn our wits so upside down ? The common man can only say, " *Of course* we smile, *of course* our heart palpitates at the sight of the crowd, *of course* we love the maiden, that beautiful soul clad in that perfect form, so palpably and flagrantly made from all eternity to be loved " (W. James, " Principles of Psychology " vol. ii. p. 386).

whether all decisions having this form must be looked upon as essentially of instinctive origin. Inquiry, however, reveals the fact that the bulk of opinion based upon assumptions having these introspectual characters is so vast that any answer but a negative one would seem totally incompatible with current conceptions of the nature of human thought.[1]

Many attempts have been made to explain the behaviour of man as dictated by instinct. He is, in fact, moved by the promptings of such obvious instincts as self-preservation, nutrition, and sex enough to render the enterprise hopeful and its early spoils enticing. So much can so easily be generalized under these three impulses that the temptation to declare that all human behaviour could be resumed under them was irresistible. These early triumphs of materialism soon, however, began to be troubled by doubt. Man, in spite of his obvious duty to the contrary, would continue so often not to preserve himself, not to nourish himself and to prove resistant to the blandishments of sex, that the attempt to squeeze his behaviour into these three categories began to involve an increasingly obvious and finally intolerable amount of pushing and pulling, as well as so much pretence that he was altogether " in,"

[1] This introspectual quality of the " *a priori* synthesis of the most perfect sort " is found, for example, in the assumptions upon which is based the bulk of opinion in matters of Church and State, the family, justice, probity, honour, purity, crime, and so forth. Yet clearly we cannot say that there is a specific instinct concerned with each of these subjects, for that, to say the least, would be to postulate an unimaginable multiplicity of instincts, for the most part wholly without any conceivable biological usefulness. For example, there are considerable difficulties in imagining an instinct for making people Wesleyans or Roman Catholics, or an instinct for making people regard British family life as the highest product of civilization, yet there can be no question that these positions are based upon assumptions having all the characters described by James as belonging to the impulses of instinct.

when, quite plainly, so large a part of him remained
" out," that the enterprise had to be given up, and
it was once more discovered that man escaped and
must always escape any complete generalization by
science.

A more obvious inference would have been that
there was some other instinct which had not been
taken into account, some impulse, perhaps, which
would have no very evident object as regarded the
individual, but would chiefly appear as modifying
the other instincts and leading to new combinations
in which the primitive instinctive impulse was un-
recognizable as such. A mechanism such as this
very evidently would produce a series of actions
in which uniformity might be very difficult to recognize by direct observation, but in which it would
be very obvious if the characters of this unknown
" x " were available.

Now, it is a striking fact that amongst animals
there are some whose conduct can be generalized
very readily in the categories of self-preservation,
nutrition, and sex, while there are others whose
conduct cannot be thus summarized. The behaviour
of the tiger and the cat is simple, and easily
comprehensible, presenting no unassimilable anomalies, whereas that of the dog, with his conscience,
his humour, his terror of loneliness, his capacity for
devotion to a brutal master, or that of the bee, with
her selfless devotion to the hive, furnishes phenomena
which no sophistry can assimilate without the aid
of a fourth instinct. But little examination will
show that the animals whose conduct it is difficult
to generalize under the three primitive instinctive
categories are gregarious. If then it can be shown
that gregariousness is of a biological significance
approaching in importance that of the other instincts,
we may expect to find in it the source of these
anomalies of conduct, and if we can also show

2

that man is gregarious, we may look to it for the
definition of the unknown " x " which might account
for the complexity of human behaviour.

III. BIOLOGICAL SIGNIFICANCE OF GREGARIOUS-
NESS.

The animal kingdom presents two relatively
sudden and very striking advances in complexity
and in the size of the unit upon which natural selection acts unmodified. These advances consist in the
aggregation of units which were previously independent and exposed to the full normal action of
natural selection, and the two instances are, of course,
the passage from the unicellular to the multicellular,
and from the solitary to the social.

It is obvious that in the multicellular organism
individual cells lose some of the capacities of the
unicellular—reproductive capacity is regulated and
limited, nutrition is no longer possible in the old
simple way and response to stimuli comes only in
certain channels. In return for these sacrifices we
may say, metaphorically, that the action of natural
selection is withdrawn from within the commune.
Unfitness of a given cell or group of cells can be
eliminated only through its effect upon the whole
organism. The latter is less sensitive to the vagaries
of a single cell than is the organism of which
the single cell is the whole. It would seem, therefore, that there is now allowed a greater range of
variability for the individual cells, and perhaps,
therefore, an increased richness of the material to
be selected from. Variations, moreover, which were
not immediately favourable would now have a
chance of surviving.

Looked at in this way, multicellularity presents
itself as an escape from the rigour of natural selection, which for the unicellular organism had narrowed

competition to so desperate a struggle that any variation outside the straitest limits was fatal, for even though it might be favourable in one respect, it would, in so small a kingdom, involve a loss in another. The only way, therefore, for further advantageous elaboration to occur was by the enlargement of the competing unit. Various species of multicellular organisms might in time be supposed in turn to reach the limit of their powers. Competition would be at its maximum, smaller and smaller variations would be capable of producing serious results. In the species where these conditions prevail an enlargement of the unit is imminent if progress is to occur. It is no longer possible by increases of physical complexity and the apparently inevitable sequence is the appearance of gregariousness. The necessity and inevitableness of the change are shown by its scattered development in very widely separated regions (for example, in insects and in mammals) just as, we may suspect, multicellularity appeared.

Gregariousness seems frequently to be regarded as a somewhat superficial character, scarcely deserving, as it were, the name of an instinct, advantageous it is true, but not of fundamental importance or likely to be deeply ingrained in the inheritance of the species. This attitude may be due to the fact that among mammals at any rate the appearance of gregariousness has not been accompanied by any very gross physical changes which are obviously associated with it.[1]

To whatever it may be due, this method of regarding the social habit is, in the opinion of the present writer, not justified by the facts, and prevents the attainment of conclusions of considerable fruitfulness.

A study of bees and ants shows at once how

[1] Among gregarious insects there are of course physical changes arising out of and closely dependent on the social organization.

fundamental the importance of gregariousness may become. The individual in such communities is completely incapable, often physically, of existing apart from the community, and this fact at once gives rise to the suspicion that even in communities less closely knit than those of the ant and the bee, the individual may in fact be more dependent on communal life than appears at first sight.

Another very striking piece of general evidence of the significance of gregariousness as no mere late acquirement is the remarkable coincidence of its occurrence with that of exceptional grades of intelligence or the possibility of very complex re-actions to environment. It can scarcely be regarded as an unmeaning accident that the dog, the horse, the ape, the elephant, and man are all social animals. The instances of the bee and the ant are perhaps the most amazing. Here the advantages of gre-gariousness seem actually to outweigh the most prodigious differences of structure, and we find a condition which is often thought of as a mere habit, capable of enabling the insect nervous system to compete in the complexity of its power of adapta-tion with that of the higher vertebrates.

If it be granted that gregariousness is a phenome-non of profound biological significance and one likely therefore to be responsible for an important group of instinctive impulses, the next step in our argument is the discussion of the question as to whether man is to be regarded as gregarious in the full sense of the word, whether, that is to say, the social habit may be expected to furnish him with a mass of instinctive impulse as mysteriously potent as the impulses of self-preservation, nutrition, and sex. Can we look to the social instinct for an explanation of some of the " *a priori* syntheses of the most perfect sort needing no proof but their own evidence," which are not explained by the three primitive categories of instinct, and remain stumbling-blocks in the way of generalizing the conduct of man?

The conception of man as a gregarious animal is, of course, extremely familiar ; one frequently meets with it in the writings of psychologists and sociologists, and it has obtained a respectable currency with the lay public. It has, indeed, become so hackneyed that it is the first duty of a writer who maintains the thesis that its significance is not even yet fully understood, to show that the popular conception of it has been far from exhaustive. As used hitherto the idea seems to have had a certain vagueness which greatly impaired its practical value. It furnished an interesting analogy for some of the behaviour of man, or was enunciated as a half serious illustration by a writer who felt himself to be in an exceptionally sardonic vein, but it was not at all widely looked upon as a definite fact of biology, which must have consequences as precise and a significance as ascertainable as the secretion of the gastric juice or the refracting apparatus of the eye. One of the most familiar attitudes was that which regarded the social instinct as a late development. The family was looked upon as the primitive unit ; from it developed the tribe, and by the spread of family feeling to the tribe the social instinct arose. It is interesting that the psychological attack upon this position has been anticipated by sociologists and anthropologists, and that it is already being recognized that an undifferentiated horde rather than the family must be regarded as the primitive basis of human society.

The most important consequence of this vague way of regarding the social habit of man has been that no exhaustive investigation of its psychological corollaries has been carried out. When we see the enormous effect in determining conduct that the gregarious inheritance has in the bee, the ant, the horse, or the dog, it is quite plain that if the gregariousness of man had been seriously regarded as a definite fact a great amount of work would have been done in determining precisely what reactive tendencies it had marked out in man's mind. Unfortunately, the amount of precise work of this kind has been very small.

From the biological standpoint the probability of gregariousness being a primitive and fundamental quality in man seems to be considerable. As already pointed out, like the other great enlargement of the biological unit, but in a much more easily recognizable degree, it would appear to have the effect of enlarging the advantages of variation. Varieties not immediately favourable, varieties departing widely from the standard, varieties even unfavourable to the individual may be supposed to be given by it a chance of survival. Now the course of the development of man seems to present many features incompatible with its having proceeded amongst isolated individuals exposed to the unmodified action of natural selection. Changes so serious as the assumption of the upright posture, the reduction in the jaw and its musculature, the reduction in the acuity of smell and hearing, demand, if the species is to survive, either a delicacy of adjustment with the compensatingly developing intelligence so minute as to be almost inconceivable, or the existence of some kind of protective enclosure, however imperfect, in which the varying individuals were sheltered from the direct influence of natural selection. The existence of such a mechanism would compensate losses of physical strength in the individual by the greatly increased strength of the larger unit, of the unit, that is to say, upon which natural selection still acts unmodified.

A realization, therefore, of this function of gregariousness relieves us from the necessity of supposing that the double variations of diminishing physical and increasing mental capacity always occurred *pari passu*. The case for the primitiveness of the social habit would seem to be still further strengthened by a consideration of such widely aberrant developments as speech and the æsthetic activities, but a discussion of them here would involve an unnecessary indulgence of biological speculation.

IV. MENTAL CHARACTERISTICS OF THE GREGARIOUS ANIMAL.

(a) Current Views in Sociology and Psychology.

If we now assume that gregariousness may be regarded as a fundamental quality of man, it remains to discuss the effects we may expect it to have produced upon the structure of his mind. It would be well, however, first, to attempt to form some idea of how far investigation has already gone in this direction. It is of course clear that no complete review of all that has been said concerning a conception so familiar can be attempted here, and, even if it were possible, it would not be a profitable enterprise, as the great bulk of writers have not seen in the idea anything to justify a fundamental examination of it. What will be done here, therefore, will be to mention a few representative writers who have dealt with the subject, and to give in a summary way the characteristic features of their exposition.

As far as I am aware, the first person to point out any of the less obvious biological significance of gregariousness was Professor Karl Pearson.[1]

[1] Many references to the subject will be found in his published works, for example in " The Grammar of Science," in " National Life from the Standpoint of Science," and in " The Chances of Death." In the collection of Essays last named the essay entitled " Socialism and Natural Selection " deals most fully with the subject.

He called attention to the enlargement of the
selective unit effected by the appearance of gregariousness, and to the fact that therefore within
the group the action of natural selection becomes
modified. This conception had, as is well known,
escaped the insight of Haeckel, of Spencer, and
of Huxley, and Pearson showed into what confusions
in their treatment of the problems of society these
three had been led by the oversight.[1] For example
may be mentioned the famous antithesis of the
" cosmical " and the " ethical " processes expounded
in Huxley's Romanes Lecture.   It was quite definitely indicated by Pearson that the so-called ethical
process, the appearance, that is to say, of altruism,
is to be regarded as a directly instinctive product
of gregariousness, and as natural, therefore, as any
other instinct.

These very clear and valuable conceptions do not
seem, however, to have received from biologists the
attention they deserved, and as far as I am aware
their author has not continued further the examination of the structure of the gregarious mind,
which would undoubtedly have yielded in his hands
further conclusions of equal value.

We may next examine the attitude of a modern
sociologist. I have chosen for this purpose the
work of an American sociologist, Lester Ward, and
propose briefly to indicate his position as it may
be gathered from his book entitled " Pure
Sociology."[2]

[1] "Socialism and Natural Selection" in " The Chances of Death."

[2] Lester F. Ward, " Pure Sociology : a Treatise on the Origin and
Spontaneous Development of Society." New York : The Macmillan
Co. 1903. I do not venture to decide whether this work may be
regarded as representative of orthodox sociology, if there be such a
thing ; I have made the choice because of the author's capacity for
fresh and ingenious speculation and his obviously wide knowledge of
sociological literature.

The task of summarizing the views of any sociologist seems to me to be rendered difficult by a certain vagueness in outline of the positions laid down, a certain tendency for a description of fact to run into an analogy, and an analogy to fade into an illustration. It would be discourteous to doubt that these tendencies are necessary to the fruitful treatment of the material of sociology, but, as they are very prominent in connection with the subject of gregariousness, it is necessary to say that one is fully conscious of the difficulties they give rise to, and feels that they may have led one into unintentional misrepresentation.

With this proviso it may be stated that the writings of Ward produce the feeling that he regards gregariousness as furnishing but few precise and primitive characteristics of the human mind. The mechanisms through which group " instinct " acts would seem to be to him largely rational processes, and group instinct itself is regarded as a relatively late development more or less closely associated with a rational knowledge that it " pays." For example, he says : " For want of a better name, I have characterized this social instinct, or instinct of race safety, as religion, but not without clearly perceiving that it constitutes the primordial undifferentiated plasm out of which have subsequently developed all the more important human institutions. This . . . if it be not an instinct, is at least the human homologue of animal instinct, and served the same purpose *after the instincts had chiefly disappeared*, and when the egotistic reason would otherwise have rapidly, carried the race to destruction in its mad pursuit of pleasure for its own sake." [1]

That gregariousness has to be considered amongst

[1] " Pure Sociology," p. 134. Italics not in original. Passages of a similar tendency will be found on pp. 200 and 556.

the factors shaping the tendencies of the human mind has long been recognized by the more empirical psychologists. In the main, however, it has been regarded as a quality perceptible only in the characteristics of actual crowds—that is to say, assemblies of persons being and acting in association. This conception has served to evoke a certain amount of valuable work in the observation of the behaviour of crowds.[1]

Owing, however, to the failure to investigate as the more essential question the effects of gregariousness in the mind of the normal individual man, the theoretical side of crowd psychology has remained incomplete and relatively sterile.

There is, however, one exception, in the case of the work of Boris Sidis. In a book entitled " The Psychology of Suggestion "[2] he has described certain psychical qualities as necessarily associated with the social habit in the individual as in the crowd. His position, therefore, demands some discussion. The fundamental element in it is the conception of the normal existence in the mind of a subconscious self. This subconscious or subwaking self is regarded as embodying the " lower " and more obviously brutal qualities of man. It is irrational, imitative, credulous, cowardly, cruel, and lacks all individuality, will, and self-control.[3] This personality takes the place of the normal personality during hypnosis and when the individual is one of an active crowd, as, for example, in riots, panics, lynchings, revivals, and so forth.

[1] For example, the little book of Gustave Le Bon—"Psychologie des Foules," Paris : Felix Alcan— In which are formulated many generalizations.

[2] "The Psychology of Suggestion : a Research into the Subconscious Nature of Man and Society," by Boris Sidis, with an Introduction by Prof. Wm. James. New York. 1903.

[3] " Psychology of Suggestion," p. 295.

Of the two personalities—the subconscious and the normal—the former alone is suggestible ; the successful operation of suggestion implies the recurrence, however transient, of a disaggregation of personality, and the emergence of the subwaking self as the controlling mind (pp. 89 and 90). It is this suggestibility of the subwaking self which enables man to be a social animal. " Suggestibility is the cement of the herd, the very soul of the primitive social group. . . . Man is a social animal, no doubt, but he is social because he is suggestible. Suggestibility, however, requires disaggregation of consciousness, hence society presupposes a cleavage of the mind. Society and mental epidemics are intimately related ; for the social gregarious self is the suggestible subconscious self " (p. 310).

Judged from our present standpoint, the most valuable feature of Sidis's book is that it calls attention to the undoubtedly intimate relation between gregariousness and suggestibility. The mechanism, however, by which he supposes suggestibility to come into action is more open to criticism. The conception of a permanent subconscious self is one to which it is doubtful whether the evidence compels assent.[1] The essential difference, however, which Sidis's views present from those to be developed below, lies in his regarding suggestibility as being something which is liable to intrude upon the normal mind as the result of a disaggregation of consciousness, instead of as a necessary, quality of every normal mind, continually, present, and an inalienable accompaniment of human thought. A careful reading of his book gives a very clear impression that he looks upon suggestibility as a

[1] In this connexion the " Symposium on the Subconscious " in the *Journal of Abnormal Psychology*, vol. ii. Nos. 1 and 2, is of much interest. The discussion is contributed to by Münsterberg, Ribot Jastrow, Pierre Janet, and Morton Prince

disreputable and disastrous legacy of the brute and the savage, undesirable in civilized life, opposed to the satisfactory development of the normal individuality, and certainly in no way associated at its origin with a quality so valuable as altruism. Moreover, one gets the impression that he regards suggestibility as being manifested chiefly, if not solely, in crowds, in panics, revivals, and in conditions generally in which the element of close association is well marked.

(*b*) Deductive Considerations

The functions of the gregarious habit in a species may broadly be defined as offensive or defensive, or both. Whichever of these modes it has assumed in the animal under consideration, it will be correlated with effects which will be divisible into two classes—the general characteristics of the social animal, and the special characteristics of the form of social habit possessed by the given animal. The dog and the sheep illustrate well the characteristics of the two simple forms of gregariousness—offensive and defensive.

1. *Special Characteristics of the Gregarious Animal.*

These need not be dealt with here, as they are the qualities which for the most part have been treated of by psychologists in such work as has been done on the corollaries of gregariousness in man. This is because they are qualities which are most evident in man's behaviour when he acts in crowds, and are then evident as something temporarily superadded to the possibilities of the isolated individual. Hence it has come about that they have been taken for the most part as constituting the whole of man's gregarious inheritance, while the possibility that that inheritance might have equally important consequences for the individual has been relatively neglected.

2. *General Characteristics of the Gregarious Animal.*

The cardinal quality of the herd is homogeneity. It is clear that the great advantage of the social habit is to enable large numbers to act as one, whereby in the case of the hunting gregarious animal strength in pursuit and attack is at once increased to beyond that of the creatures preyed upon,[1] and in protective socialism the sensitiveness of the new unit to alarms is greatly in excess of that of the individual member of the flock.

To secure these advantages of homogeneity, it is evident that the members of the herd must possess sensitiveness to the behaviour of their fellows. The individual isolated will be of no meaning, the individual as part of the herd will be capable of transmitting the most potent impulses. Each member of the flock tending to follow its neighbour and in turn to be followed, each is in some sense capable of leadership ; but no lead will be followed that departs widely from normal behaviour. A lead will be followed only from its resemblance to the normal. If the leader go so far ahead as definitely to cease to be in the herd, he will necessarily be ignored.

The original in conduct, that is to say resistiveness to the voice of the herd, will be suppressed

[1] The wolf pack forms an organism, it is interesting to note, stronger than the lion or the tiger ; capable of compensating for the loss of members ; inexhaustible in pursuit, and therefore capable by sheer strength of hunting down without wile or artifice the fleetest animals ; capable finally of consuming all the food it kills, and thus possessing another considerable advantage over the large solitary carnivora in not tending uselessly to exhaust its food supply. The advantages of the social habit in carnivora is well shown by the survival of wolves in civilized countries even to-day.

by natural selection ; the wolf which does not follow the impulses of the herd will be starved ; the sheep which does not respond to the flock will be eaten.

Again, not only will the individual be responsive to impulses coming from the herd, but he will treat the herd as his normal environment. The impulse to be in and always to remain with the herd will have the strongest instinctive weight. Anything which tends to separate him from his fellows, as soon as it becomes perceptible as such, will be strongly resisted.

So far, we have regarded the gregarious animal objectively. We have seen that he behaves as if the herd were the only environment in which he can live, that he is especially sensitive to impulses coming from the herd, and quite differently affected by the behaviour of animals not in the herd. Let us now try to estimate the mental aspects of these impulses. Suppose a species in possession of precisely the instinctive endowments which we have been considering, to be also self-conscious, and let us ask what will be the forms under which these phenomena will present themselves in its mind. In the first place, it is quite evident that impulses derived from herd feeling will enter the mind with the value of instincts—they will present themselves as " *a priori* syntheses of the most perfect sort needing no proof but their own evidence." They will not, however, it is important to remember, necessarily always give this quality to the same specific acts, but will show this great distinguishing characteristic that they may give to *any opinion whatever* the characters of instinctive belief, making it into an " *a priori synthesis* " ; so that we shall expect to find acts which it would be absurd to look upon as the results of specific instincts carried out with all the enthusiasm of instinct, and displaying all the marks of instinctive behaviour. The failure to recognize this appearance of herd impulse as a tendency, as a power which can confer instinctive sanctions on any part of the field of belief or action, has prevented the social habit of man from attracting as much of the attention of psychologists as it might profitably have done.

In interpreting into mental terms the consequences of gregariousness, we may conveniently begin with the simplest. The conscious individual will feel an unanalysable primary sense of comfort in the actual presence of his fellows, and a similar sense of discomfort in their absence. It will be obvious truth to him that it is not good for the man to be alone. Loneliness will be a real terror, insurmountable by reason.

Again, certain conditions will become secondarily associated with presence with, or absence from, the herd. For example, take the sensations of heat and cold. The latter is prevented in gregarious animals by close crowding, and experienced in the reverse condition ; hence it comes to be connected in the mind with separation, and so acquires altogether unreasonable associations of harmfulness. Similarly, the sensation of warmth is associated with feelings of the secure and salutary. It has taken medicine many thousands of years to begin to doubt the validity of the popular conception of the harmfulness of cold ; yet to the psychologist such a doubt is immediately obvious.[1]

Slightly more complex manifestations of the same tendency to homogeneity are seen in the desire for identification with the herd in matters of opinion.

[1] Any one who has watched the behaviour of the dog and the cat towards warmth and cold cannot have failed to notice the effect of the gregarious habit on the former. The cat displays a moderate liking for warmth, but also a decided indifference to cold, and will quietly sit in the snow in a way which would be impossible to the dog.

Here we find the biological explanation of the ineradicable impulse mankind has always displayed
towards segregation into classes.   Each one of us
in his opinions and his conduct, in matters of dress,
amusement, religion, and politics, is compelled to
obtain the support of a class, of a herd within the
herd.   The most eccentric in opinion or conduct
is, we may be sure, supported by the agreement
of a class, the smallness of which accounts for his
apparent eccentricity, and the preciousness of which
accounts for his fortitude in defying general opinion.
Again, anything which tends to emphasize difference
from the herd is unpleasant.   In the individual mind
there will be an unanalysable dislike of the novel
in   action   or   thought.   It   will   be   " wrong,"
" wicked," " foolish," " undesirable," or as we say
" bad form," according to varying circumstances
which we can already to some extent define.

Manifestations relatively more simple are shown
in the dislike of being conspicuous, in shyness and
in stage fright.   It is, however, sensitiveness to the
behaviour of the herd which has the most important
effects upon the structure of the mind of the gregarious   animal.   This   sensitiveness   is   closely
associated with the suggestibility of the gregarious
animal, and therefore with that of man.   The effect
of it will clearly be to make acceptable those suggestions which come from the herd, and those only.
It is of especial importance to note that this suggestibility is not general, and that it is only herd suggestions which are rendered acceptable by the action
of instinct.   Man is, for example, notoriously
insensitive to the suggestions of experience.   The
history of what is rather grandiosely called human
progress everywhere illustrates this.   If we look
back upon the development of some such thing as
the steam-engine, we cannot fail to be struck by
the extreme obviousness of each advance, and how

obstinately it was refused assimilation until the machine almost invented itself.

Again, of two suggestions, that which the more perfectly embodies the voice of the herd is the more acceptable. The chances an affirmation has of being accepted could therefore be most satisfactorily expressed in terms of the bulk of the herd by which it is backed.

It follows from the foregoing that anything which dissociates a suggestion from the herd will tend to ensure such a suggestion being rejected. For example, an imperious command from an individual known to be without authority is necessarily disregarded, whereas the same person making the same suggestion in an indirect way so as to link it up with the voice of the herd will meet with success.

It is unfortunate that in discussing these facts it has been necessary to use the word " suggestibility," which has so thorough an implication of the abnormal. If the biological explanation of suggestibility here set forth be accepted, the latter must necessarily be a normal quality of the human mind. To believe must be an ineradicable natural bias of man, or in other words an affirmation, positive or negative, is more readily accepted than rejected, unless its source is definitely dissociated from the herd. Man is not, therefore, suggestible by fits and starts, not merely in panics and in mobs, under hypnosis, and so forth, but always, everywhere, and under any circumstances. The capricious way in which man reacts to different suggestions has been attributed to variations in his suggestibility. This in the opinion of the present writer is an incorrect interpretation of the facts which are more satisfactorily explained by regarding the variations as due to the differing extent to which suggestions are identified with the voice of the herd.

Man's resistiveness to certain suggestions, and

especially to experience, as is seen so well in his
attitude to the new, becomes therefore but another
evidence of his suggestibility, since the new has
always to encounter the opposition of herd tradition.

The apparent diminution in direct suggestibility
with advancing years, such as was demonstrated
in children by Binet, is in the case of the adult
familiar to all, and is there usually regarded as
evidence of a gradually advancing organic change
in the brain.   It can be regarded, at least plausibly,
as being due to the fact that increase of years
must bring an increase in the accumulations of herd
suggestion, and so tend progressively to fix opinion.

In the early days of the human race, the appearance of the faculty of speech must have led to an
immediate increase in the extent to which the decrees
of the herd could be promulgated, and the field
to which they applied.   Now the desire for certitude
is one of profound depth in the human mind, and
possibly a necessary property of any mind, and it
is very plausible to suppose that it led in these early
days to the whole field of life being covered by
pronouncements backed by the instinctive sanction
of the herd.   The life of the individual would be
completely surrounded by sanctions of the most
tremendous kind.   He would know what he might
and might not do, and what would happen if he
disobeyed.   It would be immaterial if experience
confirmed these beliefs or not, because it would
have incomparably less weight than the voice of
the herd.   Such a period is the only trace perceptible
by the biologist of the Golden Age fabled by the
poet, when things happened as they ought, and
hard facts had not begun to vex the soul of man.
In some such condition we still find the Central
Australian native.   His whole life, to its minutest
detail, is ordained for him by the voice of the
herd, and he must not, under the most dreadful

sanctions, step outside its elaborate order. It does
not matter to him that an infringement of the code
under his very eyes is not followed by judgment,
for with tribal suggestion so compactly organized,
such cases are in fact no difficulty, and do not
trouble his belief, just as in more civilized countries
apparent instances of malignity in the reigning deity,
are not found to be inconsistent with his benevo-
lence.

Such must everywhere have been primitive human
conditions, and upon them reason intrudes as an
alien and hostile power, disturbing the perfection
of life, and causing an unending series of conflicts.

Experience, as is shown by the whole history of
man, is met by resistance because it invariably encounters decisions based upon instinctive belief, and
nowhere is this fact more clearly to be seen than
in the way in which the progress of science has
been made.

In matters that really interest him, man cannot
support the suspense of judgment which science so
often has to enjoin. He is too anxious to feel
certain to have time to know. So that we see of
the sciences, mathematics appearing first, then astro-
nomy, then physics, then chemistry, then biology,
then psychology, then sociology—but always the new
field was grudged to the new method, and we still
have the denial to sociology of the name of science.
Nowadays, matters of national defence, of politics,
of religion, are still too important for knowledge,
and remain subjects for certitude ; that is to say, in
them we still prefer the comfort of instinctive belief,
because we have not learnt adequately to value the
capacity to foretell.

Direct observation of man reveals at once the
fact that a very considerable proportion of his beliefs
are non-rational to a degree which is immediately
obvious without any special examination, and with

no special resources other than common knowledge. If we examine the mental furniture of the average man, we shall find it made up of a vast number of judgments of a very precise kind upon subjects of very great variety, complexity, and difficulty. He will have fairly settled views upon the origin and nature of the universe, and upon what he will probably call its meaning ; he will have conclusions as to what is to happen to him at death and after, as to what is and what should be the basis of conduct. He will know how the country should be governed, and why it is going to the dogs, why this piece of legislation is good and that bad. He will have strong views upon military and naval strategy, the principles of taxation, the use of alcohol and vaccination, the treatment of influenza, the prevention of hydrophobia, upon municipal trading, the teaching of Greek, upon what is permissible in art, satisfactory in literature, and hopeful in science.

The bulk of such opinions must necessarily be without rational basis, since many of them are concerned with problems admitted by the expert to be still unsolved, while as to the rest it is clear that the training and experience of no average man can qualify him to have any opinion upon them at all. The rational method adequately used would have told him that on the great majority of these questions there could be for him but one attitude—that of suspended judgment.

In view of the considerations that have been discussed above, this wholesale acceptance of non-rational belief must be looked upon as normal. The mechanism by which it is effected demands some examination, since it cannot be denied that the facts conflict noticeably with popularly current views as to the part taken by reason in the formation of opinion.

It is clear at the outset that these beliefs are invariably regarded by the holder as rational, and defended as such, while the position of one who holds contrary views is held to be obviously unreasonable. The religious man accuses the atheist of being shallow and irrational, and is met by a similar reply; to the Conservative, the amazing thing about the Liberal is his incapacity to see reason and accept the only possible solution of public problems. Examination reveals the fact that the differences are not due to the commission of the mere mechanical fallacies of logic, since these are easily avoided, even by the politician, and since there is no reason to suppose that one party in such controversies is less logical than the other. The difference is due rather to the fundamental assumptions of the antagonists being hostile, and these assumptions are derived from herd suggestion ; to the Liberal, certain basal conceptions have acquired the quality of instinctive truth, have become "*a priori* syntheses," because of the accumulated suggestions to which he has been exposed, and a similar explanation applies to the atheist, the Christian, and the Conservative. Each, it is important to remember, finds in consequence the rationality of his position flawless, and is quite incapable of detecting in it the fallacies which are obvious to his opponent, to whom that particular series of assumptions has not been rendered acceptable by herd suggestion.

To continue further the analysis of non-rational opinion, it should be observed that the mind rarely leaves uncriticized the assumptions which are forced on it by herd suggestion, the tendency being for it to find more or less elaborately rationalized justifications of them. This is in accordance with the enormously exaggerated weight which is always ascribed to reason in the formation of opinion and conduct, as is very well seen, for example, in the explanation of the existence of altruism as being due to man seeing that it " pays."

It is of cardinal importance to recognize that in this process of the rationalization of instinctive belief, it is the belief which is the primary thing, while the explanation, although masquerading as the cause of the belief, as the chain of rational evidence on which the belief is founded, is entirely secondary, and but for the belief would never have been thought of. Such rationalizations are often, in the case of intelligent people, of extreme ingenuity, and may be very misleading unless the true instinctive basis of the given opinion or action is thoroughly understood.

This mechanism enables the English lady, who, to escape the stigma of having normal feet, subjects them to a formidable degree of lateral compression, to be aware of no logical inconsequence when she subscribes to missions to teach the Chinese lady how absurd it is to compress her feet longitudinally; it enables the European lady who wears rings in her ears to smile at the barbarism of the coloured lady who wears her rings in her nose; it enables the Englishman who is amused by the African chieftain's regard for the top hat as an essential piece of the furniture of state to ignore the identity of his own behaviour when he goes to church beneath the same tremendous ensign.

The objectivist finds himself compelled to regard these and similar correspondences between the behaviour of civilized and barbarous man as no mere interesting coincidences, but as phenomena actually and in the grossest way identical, but such an attitude is possible only when the mechanism is understood by which rationalization of these customs is effected.

The process of rationalization which has just been illustrated by some of its simpler varieties is best seen on the largest scale, and in the most elaborate form, in the pseudosciences of political economy and ethics. Both of these are occupied in deriving

from eternal principles justifications for masses of
non-rational belief which are assumed to be permanent merely because they exist.   Hence the
notorious acrobatic feats of both in the face of any
considerable variation in herd belief.

It would seem that the obstacles to rational thought
which have been pointed out in the foregoing discussion have received much less attention than should
have been directed towards them.   To maintain an
attitude of mind which could be called scientific in
any complete sense, it is of cardinal importance to
recognize that belief of affirmations sanctioned by
the herd is a normal mechanism of the human
mind, and goes on however much such affirmations
may be opposed by evidence, that reason cannot
enforce belief against herd suggestion, and finally
that totally false opinions may appear to the holder
of them to possess all the characters of rationally
verifiable truth, and may be justified by secondary
processes of rationalization which it may be impossible directly to combat by argument.

It should be noticed, however, that verifiable
truths may acquire the potency of herd suggestion,
so that the suggestibility of man does not necessarily or always act against the advancement of
knowledge.   For example, to the student of biology
the principles of Darwinism may acquire the force
of herd suggestion through being held by the
class which he most respects, is most in contact
with and the class which has therefore acquired
suggestionizing power with him.   Propositions consistent with these principles will now necessarily
be more acceptable to him, whatever the evidence
by which they are supported, than they would be
to one who had not been exposed to the same
influences.   The opinion, in fact, may be hazarded
that the acceptance of any proposition is invariably
the resultant of suggestive influences, whether the

proposition be true or false, and that the balance of suggestion is usually on the side of the false, because, education being what it is, the scientific method—the method, that is to say, of experience —has so little chance of acquiring suggestionizing force.

Thus far sensitiveness to the herd has been discussed in relation to its effect upon intellectual processes. Equally important effects are traceable in feeling.

It is obvious that when free communication is possible by speech, the expressed approval or disapproval of the herd will acquire the qualities of identity or dissociation from the herd respectively. To know that he is doing what would arouse the disapproval of the herd will bring to the individual the same profound sense of discomfort which would accompany actual physical separation, while to know that he is doing what the herd would approve will give him the sense of rightness, of gusto, and of stimulus which would accompany physical presence in the herd and response to its mandates. In both cases it is clear that no actual expression by the herd is necessary to arouse the appropriate feelings, which would come from within and have, in fact, the qualities which are recognized in the dictates of conscience. Conscience, then, and the feelings of guilt and of duty are the peculiar possessions of the gregarious animal. A dog and a cat caught in the commission of an offence will both recognize that punishment is coming ; but the dog, moreover, knows that he has done *wrong*, and he will come to be punished, unwillingly it is true, and as if dragged along by some power outside him, while the cat's sole impulse is to escape. The rational recognition of the sequence of act and punishment is equally clear to the gregarious and to the solitary animal, but it is the former only who understands that he has committed a *crime*, who has, in fact, the *sense of sin*. That this is the origin of what we call conscience is confirmed by the characteristics of the latter which are accessible to observation. Any detailed examination of the phenomena of conscience would lead too far to be admissible here. Two facts, however, should be noticed. First, the judgments of conscience vary in different circles, and are dependent on local environments ; secondly, they are not advantageous to the species to the slightest degree beyond the dicta of the morals current in the circle in which they originate. These facts—stated here in an extremely summary way— demonstrate that conscience is an indirect result of the gregarious instinct, and is in no sense derived from a special instinct forcing men to consider the good of the race rather than individual desires.

1908

SOCIOLOGICAL APPLICATIONS OF THE
PSYCHOLOGY OF HERD INSTINCT

IT was shown in the previous essay, that the gregarious mental character is evident in man's behaviour, not only in crowds and other circumstances of actual association, but also in his behaviour as an individual, however isolated. The conclusions were arrived at that man's suggestibility, is not the abnormal casual phenomenon it is often supposed to be, but a normal instinct present in every, individual, and that the apparent inconstancy, of its action is due to the common failure to recognize the extent of the field over which suggestion acts ; that the only, medium in which man's mind can function satisfactorily is the herd, which therefore is not only, the source of his opinions, his credulities, his disbeliefs, and his weaknesses, but of his altruism, his charity, his enthusiasms, and his power.

The subject of the psychological effects of herd instinct is so wide that the discussion of it in the former essay covered only a comparatively small part of the field, and that in a very, cursory way. Such as it was, however, it cannot be further amplified here, where an attempt will rather be made to sketch some of the practical corollaries of such generalizations as were laid down there.

In the first place, it must be stated with emphasis that deductive speculation of this sort finds its principal value in opening up new possibilities for the application of a more exact method'. Science is measurement, but the deductive method may indicate those things which can be most profitably measured.

When the overwhelming importance of the suggestibility of man is recognized our first effort should be to obtain exact numerical expressions of it. This is not the place to attempt any exposition of the directions in which experiment should proceed ; but it may be stated that what we want to know is, how much suggestion can do in the way of inducing belief, and it may be guessed that we shall ultimately be able to express the force of suggestion in terms of the number of undifferentiated units of the herd it represents. In the work that has already been done, chiefly by Binet and by Sidis, the suggestive force experimented with was relatively feeble, and the effects consequently were rendered liable to great disturbance from the spontaneous action of other forces of suggestion already in the mind. Sidis, for example, found that his subjects often yielded to his suggestions out of " politeness " ; this source of difficulty was obviously due to his use of pure individual suggestion, a variety which theory shows to be weak or even directly resisted.

The next feature of practical interest is connected with the hypothesis, which we attempted in the former article to demonstrate, that irrational belief forms a large bulk of the furniture of the mind, and is indistinguishable by the subject from rational verifiable knowledge. It is obviously of cardinal importance to be able to effect this distinction, for it is the failure to do so which, while it is not the cause of the slowness of advance in knowledge, is the mechanism by which this delay is brought about. Is there, then, we may ask, any discoverable touchstone by which non-rational opinion may be distinguished from rational ? Non-rational judgments, being the product of suggestion, will have the quality of instinctive opinion, or, as we may call it, of belief in the strict sense. The essence of this quality is obviousness ; the truth held in this way is one of James's "*a priori* syntheses of the most perfect sort " ; to question it is to the believer to carry scepticism to an insane degree, and will be met by contempt, disapproval, or condemnation, according to the nature of the belief in question. When, therefore, we find ourselves entertaining an opinion about the basis of which there is a quality of feeling which tells us that to inquire into it would be absurd, obviously unnecessary, unprofitable, undesirable, bad form, or wicked, we may know that that opinion is a non-rational one, and probably, therefore, founded upon inadequate evidence.

Opinions, on the other hand, which are acquired as the result of experience alone do not possess this quality of primary certitude. They are true in the sense of being verifiable, but they are unaccompanied by that profound feeling of truth which belief possesses, and, therefore, we have no sense of reluctance in admitting inquiry into them. That heavy bodies tend to fall to the earth and that fire burns fingers are truths verifiable and verified every day, but we do not hold them with impassioned certitude, and we do not resent or resist inquiry into their basis ; whereas in such a question as that of the survival of death by human personality we hold the favourable or the adverse view with a quality of feeling entirely different, and of such a kind that inquiry into the matter is looked upon as disreputable by orthodox science and as wicked by orthodox religion. In relation to this subject, it may be remarked, we often see it very interestingly shown that the holders of two diametrically opposed opinions, one of which is certainly right, may both show by their attitude that the belief is held instinctively and non-rationally, as, for example, when an atheist and a Christian unite in repudiating inquiry into the existence of the soul.

A third practical corollary of a recognition of the true gregariousness of man is the very obvious one that it is not by any means necessary that suggestion should always act on the side of unreason. The despair of the reformer has always been the irrationality of man, and latterly some have come to regard the future as hopeless until we can breed a rational species. Now, the trouble is not irrationality, not a definite preference for unreason, but suggestibility—that is, a capacity for accepting reason or unreason if it comes from the proper source.

This quality we have seen to be a direct consequence of the social habit, of a single definite instinct, that of gregariousness, the same instinct which makes social life at all possible and altruism a reality.

It does not seem to have been fully understood that if you attack suggestibility by selection—and that is what you do if you breed for rationality—you are attacking gregariousness, for there is at present no adequate evidence that the gregarious instinct is other than a simple character and one which cannot be split up by the breeder. If, then, such an effort in breeding were successful, we should exchange the manageable unreason of man for the inhuman rationality of the tiger.

The solution would seem rather to lie in seeing to it that suggestion always acts on the side of reason ; if rationality were once to become really respectable, if we feared the entertaining of an unverifiable opinion with the warmth with which we fear using the wrong implement at the dinner table, if the thought of holding a prejudice disgusted us as does a foul disease, then the dangers of man's suggestibility would be turned into advantages. We

have seen that suggestion already, has begun to
act on the side of reason in some small part of the
life of the student of science, and it is possible that
a highly sanguine prophetic imagination might detect
here a germ of future changes.

Again, a fourth corollary of gregariousness in man
is the fact expounded many years ago by Pearson
that human altruism is a natural instinctive product.
The obvious dependence of the evolution of altruism
upon increase in knowledge and inter-communica-
tion has led to its being regarded as a late and a
conscious development—as something in the nature
of a judgment by the individual that it pays him
to be unselfish. This is an interesting rationalization
of the facts because in the sense in which " pay "
is meant it is so obviously false. Altruism does
not at present, and cannot, pay, the individual in
anything but feeling, as theory declares it must.
It is clear, of course, that as long as altruism is
regarded as in the nature of a judgment, the fact
is overlooked that necessarily its only reward can
be in feeling. Man is altruistic because he must
be, not because reason recommends it, for herd
suggestion opposes any advance in altruism, and
when it can the herd executes the altruist, not of
course as such but as an innovator. This is a
remarkable instance of the protean character of the
gregarious instinct and the complexity it introduces
into human affairs, for we see one instinct producing
manifestations directly hostile to each other—
prompting to ever advancing developments of
altruism, while it necessarily leads to any new product of advance being attacked. It shows, moreover, as will be pointed out again later, that a
gregarious species rapidly developing a complex
society can be saved from inextricable confusion
only by the appearance of reason and the application
of it to life.

When we remember the fearful repressing force which society has always exercised on new forms of altruism and how constantly the dungeon, the scaffold, and the cross have been the reward of the altruist, we are able to get some conception of the force of the instinctive impulse which has triumphantly defied these terrors, and to appreciate in some slight degree how irresistible an enthusiasm it might become if it were encouraged by the unanimous voice of the herd.

In conclusion we have to deal with one more consequence of the social habit in man, a consequence the discussion of which involves some speculation of a necessarily quite tentative kind.

If we look in a broad, general way at the four instincts which bulk largely in man's life, namely, those of self-preservation, nutrition, sex, and the herd, we shall see at once that there is a striking difference between the mode of action of the first three and that of the last. The first three, which we may, for convenience and without prejudice, call the primitive instincts, have in common the characteristic of attaining their maximal activities only over short periods and in special sets of circumstances, and of being fundamentally pleasant to yield to. They do not remain in action concurrently, but when the circumstances are appropriate for the yielding to one, the others automatically fall into the background, and the governing impulse is absolute master. Thus these instincts cannot be supposed at all frequently to conflict amongst themselves, and the animal possessing them alone, however highly developed his consciousness might be, would lead a life emotionally quite simple, for at any given moment he would necessarily be doing what he most wanted to do. We may, therefore, imagine him to be endowed with the feelings of free-will and reality to a superb degree, wholly unperplexed by doubt and wholly secure in his unity of purpose.

The appearance of the fourth instinct, however, introduces a profound change, for this instinct has the characteristic that it exercises a controlling power upon the individual from without. In the case of the solitary animal yielding to instinct the act itself is pleasant, and the whole creature, as it were body and soul, pours itself out in one smooth concurrence of reaction. With the social animal controlled by herd instinct it is not the actual deed which is instinctively done, but the order to do it which is instinctively obeyed. The deed, being ordained from without, may actually be unpleasant, and so be resisted from the individual side and yet be forced instinctively into execution. The instinctive act seems to have been too much associated in current thought with the idea of yielding to an impulse irresistibly pleasant to the body, yet it is very obvious that herd instinct at once introduces a mechanism by which the sanctions of instinct are conferred upon acts by no means necessarily acceptable to the body or mind. This, of course, involves an enormous increase of the range through which instinct can be made use of. Its appearance marks the beginning of the multifarious activities of man and of his stupendous success as a species ; but a spectator watching the process at its outset, had he been interested in the destiny of the race, might have felt a pang of apprehension when he realized how momentous was the divorce which had been accomplished between instinct and individual desire. Instinctive acts are still done because they are based on " *a priori* syntheses of the most perfect sort," but they are no longer necessarily pleasant. Duty has first appeared in the world, and with it the age-long conflict which is described in the memorable words of Paul : " I delight in the law of God after the inward man ; but I see another law in my members

warring against the law of my mind and bringing
me into captivity to the law of sin which is in
my members."

Into the features and consequences of this conflict it is now necessary for us to probe a little
farther.

The element of conflict in the normal life of all
inhabitants of a civilized state is so familiar that no
formal demonstration of its existence is necessary.
In childhood the process has begun. The child
receives from the herd the doctrines, let us say,
that truthfulness is the most valuable of all the
virtues, that honesty is the best policy, that to the
religious man death has no terrors, and that there
is in store a future life of perfect happiness and
delight. And yet experience tells him with persistence that truthfulness as often as not brings him
punishment, that his dishonest playfellow has as
good if not a better time than he, that the religious
man shrinks from death with as great a terror as
the unbeliever, is as broken-hearted by bereave-
ment, and as determined to continue his hold upon
this imperfect life rather than trust himself to what
he declares to be the certainty of future bliss. To
the child, of course, experience has but little suggestive force, and he is easily consoled by the perfunctory rationalizations offered him as explanations by
his elders. Yet who of us is there who cannot
remember the vague feeling of dissatisfaction, the
obscure and elusive sense of something being wrong,
which is left by these and similar conflicts?

When the world begins to open out before us
and experience to flow in with rapidly increasing
volume, the state of affairs necessarily becomes more
obvious. The mental unrest which we, with a certain
cynicism, regard as normal to adolescence is evidence
of the heavy handicap we lay upon the developing
mind in forcing it to attempt to assimilate with

4

experience the dicta of herd suggestion. Moreover, let us remember, to the adolescent experience is no longer the shadowy and easily manipulable series of dreams which it usually is to the child. It has become touched with the warmth and reality of instinctive feeling. The primitive instincts are now fully developed and finding themselves balked at every turn by herd suggestion ; indeed, even products of the latter are in conflict among themselves. Not only sex, self-preservation, and nutrition are at war with the pronouncements of the herd, but altruism, the ideal of rationality, the desire for power, the yearning for protection, and other feelings which have acquired instinctive force from group suggestion.

The sufferings entailed by this condition are commonplace knowledge, and there is scarcely a novelist who has not dealt with them. It is around matters of sex and of religion that the conflict is most severe, and while it is no part of our purpose to make any detailed survey of the condition, it may be of interest to point out some of the more obvious significances of this localization.

Religion has always been to man an intensely serious matter, and when we realize its biological significance we can see that this is due to a deeply ingrained need of his mind. The individual of a gregarious species can never be truly independent and self-sufficient. Natural selection has ensured that as an individual he must have an abiding sense of incompleteness, which, as thought develops in complexity, will come to be more and more abstractly expressed. This is the psychological germ which expresses itself in the religious feelings, in the desire for completion, for mystical union, for incorporation with the infinite, which are all provided for in Christianity and in all the successful sub-varieties of Christianity which modern times have

seen develop. This need seems with the increasing
complexity of society to become more and more
imperious, or rather to be satisfiable only by
more and more elaborately rationalized expressions.
The following is a representative passage from a
recent very popular book of mystical religion :
" The great central fact in human life, in your life
and in mine, is the coming into a conscious vital
realization of our oneness with the Infinite Life and
the opening of ourselves fully to this divine inflow."
It is very interestingly shown here to what lengths
of rationalization may be forced the consequences
of that yearning in us which is identical with the
mechanism that binds the wolf to the pack, the sheep
to the flock, and to the dog makes the company
of his master like walking with God in the cool of
the evening.

Did an opportunity offer, it would be interesting
to inquire into the relation of the same instinctive
impulse to the genesis of philosophy. Such an
attempt would, however, involve too great a
digression from the argument of this essay.

That sex should be a chief field for the conflicts
we are discussing is comprehensible not only from
the immense strength of the impulse and the fact
that it is a mode of man's activity which herd
suggestion has always tried to regulate, but also
because there is reason to believe that the sex
impulse becomes secondarily associated with another
instinctive feeling of great strength, namely,
altruism. We have seen already that altruism is
largely antagonized by herd tradition, and it is
plausible to suppose that the overwhelming rush
of this feeling which is usually associated with sex
feelings is not altogether sexual in quality, but
secondarily associated therewith as being the only
outlet through which it is allowed by the herd to
indulge manifestations of really passionate intensity.

If this were so it would clearly be of great practical importance should the rational method ever come to be applied to the solution of the problems for the sociologist and statesman which surround the relations of the sexes.

The conflicts which we are discussing are of course by no means limited to the periods of childhood and adolescence, but are frequently carried over into adult life. To understand how the apparent calm of normal adult life is attained, it is necessary to consider the effects upon the mind of these processes of contention.

Let us consider the case of a person caught in one of those dilemmas which society presents so abundantly to its members—a man seized with a passion for some individual forbidden to him by the herd, or a man whose eyes have been opened to the vision of the cruelty which everywhere lies close below the surface of life, and yet has deeply ingrained in him the doctrine of the herd that things, on the whole, are fundamentally right, that the universe is congruous with his moral feelings, that the seeming cruelty is mercy and the apparent indifference long-suffering. Now, what are the possible developments in such a tormented soul?

The conflict may end through the subsidence of either antagonist. Years, other instincts, or grosser passions may moderate the intensity of ungratified love or take away the sharpness from the sight of incomprehensible pain.

Again, scepticism may detect the nature of the herd suggestion and deprive it of its compelling force.

Thirdly, the problem may be shirked by the easy, mechanism of rationalization. The man may take his forbidden pleasure and endow a chapel, persuading himself that his is a special case, that at any rate he is not as bad as X, or, Y, or Z, who

committed such and such enormities, that after all
there is Divine mercy, and he never beat his wife,
and was always regular with his subscriptions to
missions and the hospitals. Or, if his difficulty
is the ethical one, he will come to see how right
the herd view really is ; that it is a very narrow
mind which cannot see the intrinsic excellence of
suffering ; that the sheep and cattle we breed for
eating, the calf we bleed to death that its meat may
be white, the one baby out of four we kill in the
first year of life, that cancer, consumption, and
insanity and the growing river of blood which bathes
the feet of advancing mankind, all have their part
in the Increasing Purpose which is leading the race
ever upwards and onwards to a Divine consummation of joy. Thus the conflict ceases, and the
man is content to watch the blood and the Purpose
go on increasing together and to put on flesh unperplexed by the shallow and querulous scruples of
his youth.

Of these three solutions that of scepticism is
unquestionably the least common, though the impression that this is not the case is created by the
frequency of apparent scepticism, which, in fact,
merely masks the continuation of conflict in the
deeper strata of the mind. A man the subject of
such submerged conflict, though he may appear to
others, and, of course, to himself, to have reached
a secure and uncontested basis of stability, may,
after a period of apparently frictionless mental life,
betray by unmistakable evidence the fact that conflict has continued disastrously below the surface.

The solutions by indifference and by rationalization or by a mixture of these two processes are
characteristic of the great class of normal, sensible,
reliable middle age, with its definite views, its
resiliency to the depressing influence of facts, and
its gift for forming the backbone of the State. In

them herd suggestion shows its capacity to triumph over experience, to delay the evolution of altruism, and to obscure the existence and falsify the results of the contest between personal and social desires. That it is able to do so has the advantage of establishing existing society with great firmness, but it has also the consequence of entrusting the conduct of the State and the attitude of it towards life to a class which their very stability shows to possess a certain relative incapacity to take experience seriously, a certain relative insensibility to the value of feeling and to suffering, and a decided preference for herd tradition over all other sources of conduct.

Early in history the bulk of mankind must have been of this type, because experience, being still relatively simple, would have but little suggestive force, and would therefore readily be suppressed by herd suggestion. There would be little or no mental conflict, and such as there was would be readily stilled by comparatively simple rationalizations. The average man would then be happy, active, and possessed of an inexhaustible fund of motive and energy, capable of intense patriotism and even of self-immolation for the herd. The nation consequently, in an appropriate environment, would be an expanding one and rendered ruthless and formidable by an intense, unshakable conviction of its divine mission. Its blindness towards the new in experience would keep its patriots narrow and fierce, its priests bigoted and bloodthirsty, its rulers arrogant, reactionary, and over-confident. Should chance ordain that there arose no great environmental change rendering necessary great modifications, such a nation would have a brilliant career of conquest as has been so often demonstrated by history.

Amongst the first-class Powers to-day the mentally stable are still the directing class, and their characteristic tone is discernible in national attitudes towards experience, in national ideals and religions, and in national morality. It is this possession of the power of directing national opinion by, a class which is in essence relatively insensitive towards new combinations of experience; this persistence of a mental type which may have been adequate in the simpler past, into a world where environments are daily becoming more complex—it is this survival, so to say, of the waggoner upon the footplate of the express engine, which has made the modern history of nations a series of such breathless adventures and hairbreadth escapes. To those who are able to view national affairs from an objective standpoint, it is obvious that each of these escapes might very easily have been a disaster, and that sooner or later one of them must be such.

Thus far we have seen that the conflict between herd suggestion and experience is associated with the appearance of the great mental type which is commonly called normal. Whether or not it is in fact to be regarded as such is comparatively unimportant and obviously, a question of statistics; what is, however, of an importance impossible to exaggerate is the fact that in this type of mind personal satisfactoriness or adequacy, or, as we may call it, mental comfort, is attained at the cost of an attitude towards experience which greatly affects the value to the species of the activities of minds of this type. This mental stability, then, is to be regarded as, in certain important directions, a loss; and the nature of the loss resides in a limitation of outlook, a relative intolerance of the new in thought, and a consequent narrowing of the range of facts over which satisfactory intellectual activity is possible. We may, therefore, for convenience, refer to this type as the resistive, a name which serves as a reminder of the exceedingly important fact that,

however " normal " the type may be, it is one which
falls far short of the possibilities of the human
mind.

If we now turn to a consideration of the mental
characteristics of the constituents of society other
than those of the resistive type, we shall find a
common quality traceable, and another great type
capable of broad definition. We must at once,
however, guard ourselves against being misled by the
name " normal " as applied to the resistant into the
supposition that this type is in a numerical majority
in society. Intellectually unquestionably of inferior
value, there is good reason to suppose that in mere
numbers it has already passed its zenith, as may be
gathered from the note of panic which what is
called the increase of degeneracy is beginning to
excite.

Outside the comfortable and possibly diminishing
ranks of the " normal," society is everywhere
penetrated by a steadily increasing degree of what
we may call in the broadest possible way mental
instability. All observers of society, even the most
optimistic, are agreed that the prevalence of this
mental quality is increasing, while those who are
competent to trace its less obtrusive manifestations find it to be very widespread.

When the twenty years just past come to be
looked back upon from the distant future, it is
probable that their chief claim to interest will be
that they saw the birth of the science of abnormal
psychology. That science, inconspicuous as has
been its development, has already given us a few
generalizations of the first importance. Amongst
such, perhaps the most valuable is that which has
taught us that certain mental and physical manifestations which have usually been regarded as
disease in the ordinary sense are due to the effects
upon the mind of the failure to assimilate the

experience presented to it into a harmonious unitary, personality. We have seen that the stable-minded deal with an unsatisfactory piece of experience by rejecting its significance. In certain minds such successful exclusion does not occur, and the unwelcome experience persists as an irritant, so to say, capable neither of assimilation nor rejection. Abnormal psychology discloses the fact that such minds are apt to develop the supposed diseases we have just referred to, and the fact that these and other manifestations of what we have called mental instability are the consequences of mental conflict.

Now, we have already seen that a gregarious animal, unless his society is perfectly organized, must be subject to lasting and fierce conflict between experience and herd suggestion.[1] It is natural, therefore, to assume that the manifestations of mental instability are not diseases of the individual in the ordinary sense at all, but inevitable consequences of man's biological history and exact measures of the stage now reached of his assimilation into the gregarious life. The manifestations of mental instability and disintegration were at first supposed to be of comparatively rare occurrence and limited to certain well-known " diseases," but they are coming to be recognized over a larger and larger field, and in a great variety of phenomena.

Conditions which at first sight give rise to no suspicion of being acquired injuries to the mind, when they are looked at in the light of the facts we have been considering, reveal themselves as being scars inflicted by conflict as certainly as are some

---

[1] The word " experience " is used here in a special sense that perhaps renders necessary a word or two of definition. The experience meant is everything that comes to the individual, not only his experience of events in the external world, but also his experience of the instinctive and often egoistic impulses at work within his own personality. 1915.

forms of insanity. Characteristics which pass as vices, eccentricities, defects of temper, peculiarities of disposition, come when critically examined to be explicable as minor grades of defective mental stability, although, on account of their great frequency, they have been looked upon as normal, or at any rate in the natural order of things.

Few examples could be found to illustrate better such conditions than alcoholism. Almost universally regarded as either, on the one hand, a sin or vice, or on the other hand, as a disease, there can be little doubt that in fact it is essentially a response to a psychological necessity. In the tragic conflict between what he has been taught to desire and what he is allowed to get, man has found in alcohol, as he has found in certain other drugs, a sinister but effective peacemaker, a means of securing, for however short a time, some way out of the prison house of reality back to the Golden Age. There can be equally little doubt that it is but a comparatively small proportion of the victims of conflict who find a solace in alcohol, and the prevalence of alcoholism and the punishments entailed by the use of that dreadful remedy cannot fail to impress upon us how great must be the number of those whose need was just as great, but who were too ignorant, too cowardly, or perhaps too brave to find a release there.

We have seen that mental instability must be regarded as a condition extremely common, and produced by the mental conflict forced upon man by his sensitiveness to herd suggestion on the one hand and to experience on the other. It remains for us to estimate in some rough way the characteristics of the unstable, in order that we may be able to judge of their value or otherwise to the State and the species. Such an estimate must necessarily be exaggerated, over-sharp in its outlines, omitting

much, and therefore in many respects false. The
most prominent characteristic in which the mentally
unstable contrast with the " normal " is what we
may vaguely call motive. They tend to be weak
in energy, and especially in persistence of energy.
Such weakness may translate itself into a vague
scepticism as to the value of things in general,
or into a definite defect of what is popularly called
will power, or into many other forms, but it is
always of the same fundamental significance, for
it is always the result of the thwarting of the
primary impulses to action resident in herd suggestion by the influence of an experience which cannot
be disregarded. Such minds cannot be stimulated
for long by objects adequate to normal ambition ;
they are apt to be sceptical in such matters as
patriotism, religion, politics, social success, but the
scepticism is incomplete, so that they are readily
won to new causes, new religions, new quacks, and
as readily fall away therefrom.

We saw that the resistive gain in motive what
they lose in adaptability ; we may add that in a
sense the unstable gain in adaptability what they
lose in motive. Thus we see society cleft by the
instinctive qualities of its members into two great
classes, each to a great extent possessing what the
other lacks, and each falling below the possibilities
of human personality. The effect of the gradual
increase of the unstable in society can be seen to
a certain extent in history. We can watch it through
the careers of the Jews and of the Romans. At
first, when the bulk of the citizens were of the
stable type, the nation was enterprising, energetic,
indomitable, but hard, inelastic, and fanatically convinced of its Divine mission. The inevitable effect
of the expansion of experience which followed success
was that development of the unstable and sceptical
which ultimately allowed the nation, no longer

believing in itself or its gods, to become the almost
passive prey of more stable peoples.

In regard to the question of the fundamental
significance of the two great mental types found
in society, a tempting field for speculation at once
opens up, and many questions immediately arise
for discussion. Is, for example, the stable normal
type naturally in some special degree insensitive
to experience, and if so, is such a quality inborn or
acquired? Again, may the characteristics of the
members of this class be the result of an experience relatively easily dealt with by rationalization
and exclusion? Then again, are the unstable naturally hypersensitive to experience, or have they met
with an experience relatively difficult to assimilate?
Into the discussion of such questions we shall here
make no attempt to enter, but shall limit ourselves
to reiterating that these two types divide society
between them, that they both must be regarded as
seriously defective and as evidence that civilization
has not yet provided a medium in which the average
human mind can grow undeformed and to its full
stature.

GREGARIOUSNESS AND THE FUTURE OF MAN.

Thus far we have attempted to apply biological
conceptions to man and society as they actually exist
at present. We may now, very shortly, inquire
whether or not the same method can yield some
hint as to the course which human development
will take in the future.

As we have already seen reason to believe, in
the course of organic development when the limits
of size and efficiency in the unicellular organism
were reached, the only possible access of advantage
to the competing organism was gained by the appearance of combination. In the scale of the metazoa

we see the advantages of combination and division of labour being more and more made use of, until the individual cells lose completely the power of separate existence, and their functions come to be useful only in the most indirect way and through the organisms of which the cells are constituents. This complete submergence of the cell in the organism indicates the attainment of the maximum advantages to be obtained from this particular access in complexity, and it indicates to us the direction in which development must proceed within the limits which are produced by that other access of complexity—gregariousness.

The success and extent of such development clearly depend on the relation of two series of activities in the individual which may in the most general way be described as the capacity for varied reaction and the capacity for communication. The process going on in the satisfactorily developing gregarious animal is the moulding of the varied reactions of the individual into functions beneficial to him only indirectly through the welfare of the new unit— the herd. This moulding process is a consequence of the power of intercommunication amongst the individual constituents of the new unit. Intercommunication is thus seen to be of cardinal importance to the gregarious, just as was the nervous system to the multicellular.

Moreover, in a given gregarious species the existence of a highly developed power of reaction in the individual with a proportionately less developed capacity for communication will mean that the species is not deriving the advantages it might from the possession of gregariousness, while the full advantages of the type will be attained only when the two sets of activities are correspondingly strong.

Here we may see perhaps the explanation of the astounding success and completeness of gregarious-

ness in bees and ants. Their cycle of development was early complete because the possibilities
of reaction of the individual were so small, and
consequently the capacity for intercommunication
of the individual was relatively soon able to attain
a corresponding grade. The individual has become
as completely merged in the hive as the single
cell in the multicellular animal, and consequently
the whole of her activities is available for the uses
of the State. It is interesting to notice that, considered from this aspect, the wonderful society of
the bee, with its perfect organization and its wonderful adaptability and elasticity, owes its early
attainment of success to the smallness of the brain
power of the individual.

For the mammals with their greater powers of
varied reaction the path to the consummation of
their possibilities must be longer, more painful, and
more dangerous, and this applies in an altogether
special degree to man.

The enormous power of varied reaction possessed
by man must render necessary for his attainment of the full advantages of the gregarious
habit a power of intercommunication of absolutely
unprecedented fineness. It is clear that scarcely a
hint of such power has yet appeared, and it is
equally obvious that it is this defect which gives
to society the characteristics which are the contempt of the man of science and the disgust of
the humanitarian.

We are now in a position to understand how
momentous is the question as to what society does
with the raw material of its minds to encourage
in them the potential capacity for intercommunication which they undoubtedly by nature possess. To
that question there is but one answer. By providing
its members with a herd tradition which is constantly at war with feeling and with experience,

society drives them inevitably into resistiveness on
the one hand, or into mental instability on the
other, conditions which have this in common, that
they tend to exaggerate that isolation of the individual which is shown us by the intellect to be
unnatural and by the heart to be cruel.

Another urgent question for the future is provided by the steady increase, relative and absolute,
of the mentally unstable. The danger to the State
constituted by a large unstable class is already
generally recognized, but unfortunately realization
has so far only instigated a yet heavier blow at
the species. It is assumed that instability is a
primary quality, and therefore only to be dealt with
by breeding it out. With that indifference to the
mental side of life which is characteristic of the
mentally resistant class, the question as to the real
meaning of instability has been begged by the
invention of the disastrous word " degenerate."[1] The
simplicity of the idea has charmed modern speculation, and the only difficulty in the whole problem
has come to be the decision as to the most expe-
ditious way of getting rid of this troublesome flaw
in an otherwise satisfactory world.

The conception that the natural environment of
man must be modified if the body is to survive
has long been recognized, but the fact that the mind
is incomparably more delicate than the body has
scarcely been noticed at all. We assume that the
disorderly environment with which we surround the
mind has no effect, and are ingenuously surprised
when mental instability arises apparently from nowhere ; but although we know nothing of its origin
our temerity in applying the cure is in no sense
daunted.

It has already been pointed out how dangerous
it would be to breed man for reason—that is, against
suggestibility. The idea is a fit companion for the

device of breeding against " degeneracy." The
" degenerate "—that is, the mentally unstable—have
demonstrated by the mere fact of instability that
they possess the quality of sensitiveness to feeling
and to experience, for it is this which has prevented
them from applying the remedy of rationalization or
exclusion when they have met with experience con-
flicting with herd suggestion. There can be no
doubt as to the value to the State of such sensitiveness were it developed in a congruous environment. The " degeneracy," therefore, which we see
developed as a secondary quality in these sensitive
minds is no evidence against the degenerate, but
an indictment of the disorderly environment which
has ruined them, just as the catchword associating
insanity and genius tells us nothing about genius
but a great deal about the situation into which it
has had the misfortune to be born.

Sensitiveness to feeling and experience is undoubtedly the necessary antecedent of any high
grade of that power of intercommunication which
we have seen to be necessary to the satisfactory
development of man. Such sensitiveness, however,
in society as it now is, inevitably leads merely to
mental instability. That such sensitiveness increases
with civilization is shown by the close association
between civilization and mental instability. There
is no lack, therefore, of the mental quality of all
others most necessary to the gregarious animal.
The pressing problem which in fact faces man in
the immediate future is how to readjust the mental
environment in such a way that sensitiveness may
develop and confer on man the enormous advantages which it holds for him, without being transformed from a blessing into the curse and menace
of instability. To the biologist it is quite clear
that this can be effected only by an extension of
the rational method to the whole field of experience, a

process of the greatest difficulty, but one which must
be the next great variation in man's development if
that development is to continue to be an evolution.

Outside this possibility the imagination can see
nothing but grounds for pessimism. It needs but
little effort of foresight to realize that without some
totally revolutionary change in man's attitude towards the mind, even his very tenure of the earth
may come to be threatened. Recent developments
in the study of disease have shown us how blind and
fumbling have been our efforts against the attacks
of our immemorial enemies the unicellular organisms.
When we remember their capacities for variation
and our fixity, we can see that for the race effectually
and permanently to guard itself against even this
one danger are necessary that fineness and complexity of organization, that rendering available of
the utmost capacity of its members, against which
the face of society seems at present to be so steadily
set. We see man to-day, instead of the frank and
courageous recognition of his status, the docile attention to his biological history, the determination to
let nothing stand in the way of the security and
permanence of his future, which alone can establish
the safety and happiness of the race, substituting
blind confidence in his destiny, unclouded faith in
the essentially respectful attitude of the universe
towards his moral code, and a belief no less firm
that his traditions and laws and institutions necessarily contain permanent qualities of reality. Living
as he does in a world where outside his race no
allowances are made for infirmity, and where
figments however beautiful never become facts, it
needs but little imagination to see how great are
the probabilities that after all man will prove but
one more of Nature's failures, ignominiously to be
swept from her work-table to make way for another
venture of her tireless curiosity and patience.

1909.

5

SPECULATIONS UPON THE HUMAN MIND IN 1915

MAN'S PLACE IN NATURE AND NATURE'S PLACE IN MAN

As the nineteenth century draws away into the past and it is possible to get a comprehensive view of the intellectual legacies it has left to its successor, certain of its ideas stand out from the general mass by reason of the greatness of their scale and scope. Ideas of the first order of magnitude are from their very greatness capable of full appreciation only in a comparatively distant view. However much they have been admired and studied by contemporary thought, it is with the passage of time only that all their proportions come gradually into focus. The readjustments of thought as to what used to be called man's place in nature, which were so characteristic a work of the latter half of the nineteenth century, embodied an idea of this imperial type which, fruitful as it has proved, has even now yielded far less than its full harvest of truth.

The conception of man as an animal, at first entertained only in a narrow zoological sense, has gradually extended in significance, and is now beginning to be understood as a guiding principle in the study of all the activities of the individual and the species. In the early days such a conception was regarded by non-scientific thought as degrading to man, and as denying to him the possibility of moral progress and the reality of his higher æsthetic and emotional capabilities ; at the same time, men of science found themselves compelled, however unwillingly, to deny, that the moral activities of man could be made consistent with his status as an animal. It may, still be remembered how even the evolutionary enthusiasm of Huxley was baffled by the incompatibility he found to subsist between what he called the ethical and the cosmical processes, and how he stood bewildered by the sight of moral beauty, blossoming incorrigibly amidst the cruelty, lust, and bloodshed of the world.

The passage of time has tended more and more to clear up these lingering confusions of an anthropocentric biology, and thought is gradually gaining courage to explore, not merely the body of man but his mind and his moral capacities, in the knowledge that these are not meaningless intrusions into an otherwise orderly world, but are partakers in him and his history just as are his vermiform appendix and his stomach, and are elements in the complex structure of the universe as respectably established there, and as racy of that soil as the oldest saurian or the newest gas.

Man is thus not merely, as it were, rescued from the inhuman loneliness which he had been taught was his destiny and persuaded was his pride, but he is relieved from perplexities and temptations which had so long proved obstacles to his finding himself and setting out valiantly on an upward path. Cut off from his history and regarded as an exile into a lower world, he can scarcely fail to be appalled and crushed by the discrepancy between his lofty pretensions and his lowly acts. If he but recognize that he himself and his virtues and aspirations are integral strands in the fabric of life, he will learn that the great tissue of reality loses none of its splendour by the fact that near by where the pattern

glows with his courage and his pride it burns with
the radiance of the tiger, and over against his
intellect and his genius it mocks in the grotesques
of the ape.

The development of an objective attitude towards
the status of man has had, perhaps, its most significant effect in the influence it has exercised upon the
study of the human mind.

The desire to understand the modes of action of
the mind, and to formulate about them generalizations
which shall be of practical value, has led to inquiries
being pursued along three distinct paths. These
several methods may be conveniently distinguished
as the primitive, the human, and the comparative.

What I have called the primitive method of
psychological inquiry is also the obvious and natural
one. It takes man as it finds him, accepts his
mind for what it professes to be, and examines into
its processes by introspection of a direct and simple
kind. It is necessarily subject to the conditions
that the object of study is also the medium through
which the observations are made, and that there
is no objective standard by which the accuracy of
transmission through this medium can be estimated
and corrected. In the result the materials collected
are subjected to a very special and very stringent
kind of censorship. If an observation is acceptable
and satisfactory to the mind itself, it is reported as
true ; if it contains material which is unwelcome
to the mind, it is reported as false ; and in both
cases the failure is in no sense due to any conscious
dishonesty in the observing mind, but is a fallacy
necessarily inherent in the method. A fairly characteristic product of inquiries of this type is the conception, which seems so obvious to common sense,
that introspection does give access to all mental
processes, so that a conscious motive must be discoverable for all the acts of the subject. Experience

with more objective methods has shown that when no motive is found for a given act or no motive consistent with the mind's pretensions as to itself, there will always be a risk of a presentable one being extemporized.

Psychology of this primitive type—the naïve psychology of common sense—is always necessarily tainted with what may be called in a special sense anthropomorphism ; it tells us, that is to say, not what man is but what he thinks and feels himself to be. Judged by its fruits in enabling us to foretell or to influence conduct, it is worthless. It has been studied for thousands of years and infinite ingenuities have been expended on it, and yet at its best it can only tell us how the average man thinks his mind works—a body of information not sensibly superior in reality to the instructions of a constitutional monarch addressed to an unruly parliament. It has distracted thought with innumerable falsifications, but in all its secular cultivation has produced no body of generalizations of value in the practical conduct of life.

COMMENTS ON AN OBJECTIVE SYSTEM OF HUMAN PSYCHOLOGY

I

Until comparatively recent years the fact that what was called psychology did not even pretend to be of any practical value in affairs was tolerated by its professors and regarded as more or less in the nature of things. The science, therefore, outside a small class of specialists was in very dismal reputation. It had come to comprise two divergent schools, one which busied itself with the apparatus of the experimental physiologist and frankly studied the physiology of the nervous system, the other which occupied itself with the faded abstractions of logic and metaphysics, while both agreed in ignoring the study of the mind. This comparative sterility may in a broad way be traced back to the one fundamental defect from which the science suffered —the absence of an objective standard by which the value of mental observations could be estimated. Failing such a standard, any given mental phenomenon might be as much a product of the observing mind as of the mind observed, or the varying degrees in which both of these factors contributed might be inextricably mixed. Of late years the much-needed objective standard has been sought and to some extent found in two directions. What I have called " human " psychology has found it in the study of diseases of the mind. In states of disease mental processes and mechanisms which had eluded observation in the normal appear in an exaggerated form which renders recognition less difficult. The enlightenment coming from the understanding of such pathological material has made it possible to argue back to the less obtrusive or more effectively concealed phenomena of the normal and more or less to exclude the fallacies of the observing mind, and, at any rate in part, to dissipate the obscurity which for so long had successfully hidden the actual mental phenomena themselves.

The most remarkable attack upon the problems of psychology which has been made from the purely human standpoint is that in which the rich genius of Sigmund Freud was and still is the pioneer. The school which his work has founded was concerned at first wholly with the study of abnormal mental states, and came into notice as a branch of medicine finding the verification of its principles in the success it laid claim to in the treatment of certain mental diseases. It now regards itself as possessing a body of doctrine of general applicability to mental phenomena, normal or abnormal. These principles are the product of laborious and minute inquiries into the working of the mind, rendered possible by the use of a characteristic method known as psychoanalysis. This method, which constitutes a definite and elaborate technique of investigation, is looked upon by those who practise it as the sole means by which access can be obtained to the veritable phenomena of the mind, and as rendering possible a truly objective view of the facts. It is no part of my purpose to examine the validity of psycho-analysis as a scientific method. It is enough to notice that the exponents of it completely repudiate the teachings of what I have called " common-sense " psychology, that they maintain that objectivity in the collection and collation of psychical facts is in no way to be obtained by the light of nature but demands very special methods and precautions, and that their claims to the possession of a truly objective method appear to be open to verification or disproof by actual experiment in the treatment of disease. Whatever value, then, psycho-analysis may ultimately prove to possess in solving the peculiar difficulties of psychological research, the evolution of it marks a very definite advance in principle and shows that it is the product of a mind determined by whatever effort to get to close quarters with the facts.

The body of doctrine enunciated by Freud concerns us more directly than the peculiarities of his method. Some very general and summary account may therefore be attempted as illustrating the characteristics of this vigorous, aggressive, and essentially " human " school of research.

The Freudian psychology regards the mind of the adult as the outcome of a process of development the stages of which are within limits, orderly and inevitable. The trend of this development in each individual is determined by forces which are capable of precise definition, and the final product of it is capable of yielding to expert examination clear evidence of the particular way in which these forces have acted and interacted during the developmental process. The mind of the adult, then, is like the body in bearing traces which betray to the skilled observer the events of its developmental history. Inconspicuous and apparently insignificant structures and peculiarities in the one no less than in the other prove to have had a meaning and a function in the past, however little significance their final form may seem to possess, and thus the psychologist is able to reconstruct the history of a given subject's mind, although the most important stages of its development are hidden from direct observation as effectively, as is the prenatal growth of the body.

It seems to be a fundamental conception of the Freudian system that the development of the mind is accompanied and conditioned by mental conflict. The infant is regarded as being impelled by instinctive impulses which at first are solely egoistic. From the earliest moments of its contact with the world resistance to the full indulgence of these impulses is encountered. With the growth and intensification of such impulses, the resistance from external interference — the beginnings of social pressure—becomes more formidable, until at a quite unexpectedly early age a veritable condition of mental conflict is established—egoistic impulses fatally pressing for indulgence regardless of their acceptability to the environment, while environmental influences bear equally heavily against any indulgence unwelcome to surrounding standards of discipline, taste, or morality.

Of the two parties in this conflict—the instinctive

impulse and the repressive force—the first, according to Freud, is wholly the product of the sex
instinct. This instinct is conceived of as being
much more active and potent in the infant and
child than had been suspected by any previous investigator. The normal sexual interest and activity
as manifested in the adult are developed out of the
sexual impulse of the child by a regular series
of modifications, which appear to be regarded as
due partly to a process of natural development and
partly to the influence of external repressive forces.
In the infant the instinct is egocentric and the object
of its interest is the individual's own body ; with
the increase of the mental field consequent on
enlarging experience the instinctive activity is ex-
ternalized, and its object of interest changes so that
the child acquires a specific inclination towards other
individuals without distinction of sex ; finally, as
a last stage of development the instinctive inclination is localized to members of the opposite sex.
This series of transformations is regarded as normal
by Freud, and as essential to the appearance of the
" normal " adult type. The evolution of this series
is sensitive to interference by outside influences,
and any disturbance of it either by way of antici-
pation or delay will have profound effects upon
the ultimate character and temperament of the subject. The psychical energy of an instinct so
important as that of sex is very great, and is not
dissipated by the forces of repression brought to
bear upon it, but transformed into activities ostensibly
quite different and directed into channels having
no obvious connection with their source. It is a
fundamental characteristic of the mind to be able
to accept these substitutes for the actual indulgence
of the instinct, and to enjoy a symbolical gratification
in manifestations which have no overt sexual significance. When development proceeds normally, the

surplus energy of the sex instinct finds an outlet
in activities of social value—æsthetic, poetic, altruistic ; when development is interfered with the
outflow of energy is apt to result in definite disease
of the mind or in peculiarities of character scarcely
to be distinguished therefrom.

Thus the mind of the adult, according to Freud,
in addition to activities which are conscious and
fully accessible to the subject, carries on activities
and holds memories which are unconscious and
totally inaccessible to the subject by any ordinary,
method of introspection. Between these two fields
there is a barrier sedulously guarded by certain
repressive forces. The unconscious is the realm
of all the experiences, memories, impulses, and
inclinations which during the subject's life have
been condemned by the standards of the conscious,
have proved incompatible with it and have therefore
been outlawed from it. This banishment in no way,
deprives these excluded mental processes of their
energy, and they constantly influence the feelings
and behaviour of the subject. So strict, however,
is the guard between them and the conscious that
they are never allowed to pass the barrier between
one sphere and the other except in disguised and
fantastically distorted forms by which their true
meaning is closely concealed. It has been perhaps
Freud's most remarkable thesis that dreams are
manifestations of this emergence of desires and
memories from the unconscious into the conscious
field. During sleep the repressing force which
guards the frontier between conscious and unconscious is weakened. Even then, however, such ideas
as emerge into the conscious can do so only in a
worked up and distorted form, so that their significance can be disengaged from the grotesque
jumble of the actual dream only by a minute inquiry,
according to a difficult and highly technical method.

By this method, however, is to be obtained a deep insight into the otherwise irrecoverable emotional history of the individual, the structure of his temperament, and, if he is mentally abnormal, the meaning of his symptoms.

II

The foregoing enumeration of the chief doctrines of the Freudian psychology is intended to be no more than a mere outline to serve as a basis for certain comments which seem to be relevant to the general argument of this essay. The point of view from which this slight sketch is made, that of an interested but detached observer, is naturally somewhat different from that of the actual authorities themselves. Here it is desired to get the broadest possible view in the most general terms, and as we have no concern with immediate problems of practical therapeutics—which remain at least the chief preoccupation of writers of the psycho-analytic school—an effort has been made to avoid the use of the rich and rather forbidding technical vocabulary in which the writings of the school abound. It may well be that this generalized method of description has yielded an ill-proportioned or distorted picture. The subject has proved to be so much at the mercy of prejudice that the least impassioned spectator, however completely he may believe himself to be free from advocacy or detraction, is far from being able to claim immunity from these influences.

Keeping constantly in mind this general caution, which is at least as necessary in the field of criticism as in that of mere description, we may pass on to make certain comments on the psychology of Freud which are relevant to the general argument being followed out here.

'A discussion in any way detailed of this immense subject is very obviously impossible here, but it is desirable to say a few words as to the general validity of Freud's chief thesis. However much one may be impressed by his power as a psychologist and his almost fierce resolution to get at the actual facts of mental processes, one can scarcely fail to experience in reading Freud's works that there is a certain harshness in his grasp of facts and even a trace of narrowness in his outlook which tend to repel the least resistant mind and make one feel that his guidance in many matters—perhaps chiefly of detail—is open to suspicion. He seems to have an inclination for the enumeration of absolute rules, a confidence in his hypotheses which might be called superb if that were not in science a term of reproach, and a tendency to state his least acceptable propositions with the heaviest emphasis as if to force belief upon an unwilling and shrinking mind were an especial gratification. All these traits of manner—at the worst mere foibles of a distinguished and successful investigator—appear to exercise some considerable effect on the acceptance his writings meet with, and are perhaps indications in which direction, if he is open to fallacy, such might be looked for.

Nevertheless with regard to the main propositions of his system there can be little doubt that their *general validity* will be increasingly accepted. Among such propositions must be put the conception of the significance of mental conflict, the importance of the emotional experiences of infancy and childhood in the determination of character and the causing of mental disease, and his conception of the general structure of the mind as comprising conscious and unconscious fields.

The comments which I shall venture to make upon the work of Freud will be such as are suggested

by the biological point of view of which this essay
is intended to be an exposition. The standard of
interest upon which they are based will therefore
necessarily differ to some extent from that which
is usually adopted in writings of the psycho-analytic
school.

To the biologist perhaps the most striking
characteristic of the work of this school is its
complete acceptance of what one may call the human
point of view. It seems to be satisfied that no
useful contribution to psychology is to be obtained
outside the limits of human feeling and behaviour,
and to feel no impatience to expand its inquiries
into a still larger field. It is not that the school
has failed to show an extremely vigorous movement of expansion. Beginning as a mere province
of medicine, and while its foothold there was still
far from general recognition, it invaded the regions
of general psychology, of æsthetics, ethnology, the
study of folklore and myth, and indeed of all matters
in which it could find its essential material—the
records of human feeling and conduct. Beyond
the human species it has shown remarkably little of
this aggressive spirit, and it seems to feel no need
of bringing its principles into relation with what
little is known of the mental activities of the non-
human animals.

The absence of any strong pressure in the
direction of establishing a correlation of all mental
phenomena, whether human or not, is not a matter
of merely theoretical interest. The actual practical
success to be obtained to-day in such an attempt
might possibly be insignificant and yet of great
value in moulding the whole attitude of mind of
the investigator towards matters lying wholly within
the sphere of human psychology. However much
one may be impressed by the greatness of the edifice
which Freud has built up and by the soundness of

his architecture, one can scarcely, fail, on coming into it from the bracing atmosphere of the biological sciences, to be oppressed by, the odour of humanity, with which it is pervaded. One finds everywhere a tendency, to the acceptance of human standards and even sometimes of human pretensions which cannot fail to produce a certain uneasiness as to the validity, if not of his doctrines, at any rate of the forms in which they are expounded. The quality I am trying to describe is extremely difficult to express in concrete terms without exaggeration or distortion. To those who have approached Freud's work solely, by the path of medicine the idea that it can give any one the feeling of a certain conventionality of standard and outlook and of a certain over-estimation of the objectivity of man's moral values will seem perhaps merely absurd. That this is an impression which I have not been able altogether to escape I record with a good deal of hesitation and diffidence and without any wish to lay, stress upon it.

Psycho-analytic psychology has grown up under conditions which may, very well have encouraged the persistence of the human point of view. Originally, its whole activity was concentrated upon the investigation and treatment of disease. Many of its early disciples were those who had received proof of its value in their own persons, those, that is to say, who had been sufferers from their very susceptibility, to the influence of human standards. The objective standard of validity by which the system was judged was necessarily, that of the physician, namely the capacity to restore the abnormal mind to the " normal." Normal in this sense is of course no more than a statistical expression implying the condition of the average man. It could scarcely fail, however, to acquire the significance of " healthy." If once the statistically

normal mind is accepted as being synonymous with
the psychologically healthy mind (that is, the mind
in which the full capacities are available for use),
a standard is set up which has a most fallacious
appearance of objectivity. The statistically normal
mind can be regarded only as a mind which has
responded in the usual way to the moulding and
deforming influence of its environment—that is, to
human standards of discipline, taste, and morality.
If it is to be looked upon as typically healthy also,
the current human standards of whose influence it is
a product must necessarily be accepted as qualified
to call forth the best in the developing mind they
mould. Writers of the psycho-analytic school seem
in general to make some such assumption as this.

III

The conception of mental conflict is the central
feature of the Freudian system. Of its importance
and validity there can be no doubt. In a general
way the idea is familiar and even commonplace,
but Freud had developed it and shown how deeply
the principle penetrates the structure and development of the mind from the earliest period and to
an extent quite unsuspected by earlier psychologists.

From an early period of life the child finds the
gratification of its instinctive impulses checked or
even prevented by the pressure of its environment.
Conflict is thus set up between the two forces of
instinctive pressure within and social pressure from
without. Instinctive impulses which thus come into
conflict with the repressing force are not destroyed
but are deflected from their natural outlet, are
repressed within the mind and ultimately prevented
from rising into the conscious field at all except
in disguised or symbolic forms. To the adult his
childhood seems to have been altogether free from

any kind of sexual activity or interest, not because, as is generally supposed, such has never existed, but because it proved incapable of persisting in the conscious field and was suppressed into the unconscious with the increase of the social repressing forces. Similarly impulses experienced in adult life which are for the same reason incompatible with conscious recognition do not become conscious, but live their life in the unconscious, though they may exercise the profoundest influence on the happiness and health of the subject.

The work of Freud has been concentrated chiefly, upon the one party in these conflicts—the instinctive impulse of which the only considerable one according to him is the sexual. To the other party—the repressing forces—he has given very much less attention, and in them has found apparently much less interest. By most writers of his school also they seem to be taken very much as a matter of course.

When we consider, however, what they can accomplish—how they can take the immensely powerful instinct of sex and mould and deform its prodigious mental energy—it is clear that the repressing forces are no less important than the antagonist with which they contend.

It is desirable, perhaps, to discuss a little more closely the nature of mental conflict, and especially, first to define the precise meaning of the conception.

It may readily be granted that the young child's mind is wholly egocentric, though the proposition is not without a certain element of assumption which it is not wise altogether to ignore. He experiences certain desires and impulses which he assumes with the blandest unconsciousness of any other desires but his own are there to be gratified. The failure to gratify such an impulse may come about in several ways, not all of which are equally significant in establishing mental conflict. The gratification may be physically impossible. Here there is no basis for internal conflict. The resistance is wholly external ; the whole child still desires its pleasure and its whole resources, mental and physical, are directed to gain the object. Mere failure may be painful and may lead to an outburst of rage which possibly even discharges some of the mental energy of the wish, but the situation psychically is simple and the incident tends of itself to go no farther.

The gratification may prove to be physically painful in itself. This seems to promise certain elements of mental conflict in balancing the pleasure of the gratification against the remembered pain it involves. We are assuming that the pain is the immediate consequence of the act, as when, for example, a child makes the immemorial scientific discovery that fire burns fingers. Such a direct experience without the interposition of a second person or the pointing of a moral does not in fact involve any real mental conflict. The source of the pain is external, its only emotional quality is that of its simple unpleasantness, and this cannot, as it were, enter into the child's mind and divide it against itself.

True conflict, the conflict which moulds and deforms, must be actually within the mind—must be endopsychic to use a term invented by Freud, though not used by him in this exact application. In order that a desire may set up conflict it must be thwarted, not by a plain impossibility or by a mere physical pain, but by another impulse within the mind antagonizing it. It seems clear that the counter-impulse to be strong enough to contend with an impulse having in it the energy of the sex instinct must itself derive its force from some potent instinctive mechanism. We cannot suppose that the immense power of the sex impulse can be

6

controlled, moulded, and directed by any influence except such as have access to the stores of psychical energy which the instinctive activities alone possess.

We are thus led to the proposition that the essence of mental conflict is the antagonism of two impulses which both have instinct behind them, and are both, as it were, intimate constituents in the personality of the subject. Thus only can the mind become, in the worn but still infinitely appropriate metaphor, a house divided against itself. The counter-impulses to the developing sexual interest and activity of the child are, as we have seen, the result of social pressure—that is to say, the result of the influence of the human environment. This influence is manifested, not merely in direct precept, in warning, in punishment, in expressions of disapproval or disgust, but in the whole system of secrecy, of significant silences, of suppressions, of nods and winks and surreptitious signallings, of sudden causeless snubs and patently lame explanations amid which such sexual interest as the child possesses has to find a *modus vivendi* and an intelligible meaning.

Whence does this environmental pressure obtain the power which enables it to exercise in the child's mind the regal functions of instinct? Clearly it can do so only if the mind possesses a specific sensitiveness to external opinion and the capacity to confer on its precepts the sanction of instinctive force. In the two earlier essays of this book I attempted to show that the essential specific characteristic of the mind of the gregarious animal is this very capacity to confer upon herd opinion the psychical energy of instinct. It is this sensitiveness, then, which lays the child's mind open to the influence of his environment and endows for him the mental attitude of that environment with all the sanction of instinct. Thus do the repressing forces become actually constituent in the child's personality, and as much a part of his being as the egoistic desires with which they are now able to contend on equal terms.

The specific sensitiveness of the gregarious mind seems, then, to be a necessary condition for the establishment of true mental conflict, and a character which must be taken into account if we are to develop a complete theory of the evolution of the individual mind.

Assuming the validity of the proposition that there are two primary factors in the development of the mind in each individual—the egoistic impulses of the child and his specific sensitiveness to environing influences—it may well be asked why it is that the product, the " normal " adult mind, is so uniform in its characters. It is true that this uniformity may very easily be exaggerated, for in a very considerable number of cases gross " abnormalities " are the result of the process of development, but, as I pointed out in an earlier essay, the result on the whole is to produce two broadly distinguishable types of mind—the unstable and the stable—the latter on account of its numerical superiority being also dignified as normal A considerable uniformity in the final products must therefore be accepted. If, however, environmental influences are an essential factor in the production of this result, there seems no little difficulty in accounting for the uniformity seeing that environments vary so much from class to class, nation to nation, and race to race. Where, we may ask, is the constant in the environmental factors which the uniformity of the outcome leads us to expect? Assuming with Freud that of the egoistic impulses of the child, the sexual alone seriously counts in the formation of character, can it be shown that the influences which surround the child are uniform in their general direction against this? At first sight it would seem certainly not. Even in the same country the variations in taste, reticence, modesty, and morality towards matters of sex interest vary greatly from class to class, and presumably are accompanied by corresponding variations in the type of influence exercised by the environment of the child.

Adequately to deal with this difficulty would involve examining in detail the actual mental attitude of the adult towards the young, especially in regard to matters directly or indirectly touching upon interests of sex. The subject is a difficult one, and if we limit ourselves to the purely human standpoint, ugly and depressing. The biologist, however, need not confine himself to so cramped an outlook, and by means of collecting his observations over a much larger field is able to some extent to escape the distorting effects of natural human prejudice. Viewed in a broad way, it is neither surprising nor portentous that there should naturally exist a strong and persistent jealousy between the adult and the young. Indeed, many of the superficial consequences of this fact are mere commonplaces. Throughout most of the lower animals the relation is obvious and frankly manifested. Indeed, it may be regarded as a more or less inevitable consequence of any form of social life among animals. As such, therefore, it may be expected to appear in some form or other in the human mind. The manifestations of it, however, will by no means necessarily take easily recognizable forms. The social pressure to which the mind is subject will tend to exclude such a feeling from at any rate full consciousness, and such manifestations as are allowed it will be in disguised and distorted forms.

It seems difficult to avoid the conclusion that some dim and unrealized offshoot of such a jealousy between adult and young is responsible for the unanimity with which man combines to suppress and delay the development of any evidence of sexual interest by the young. The intensity of the dislike which is felt for admitting the young to share any part of the knowledge of the adult about the physiology of sex is well illustrated by the difficulty parents feel in communicating to their children some of the elementary facts which they may feel very strongly it is their duty to impart. A parent may find himself under these circumstances trying to quiet his conscience with all sorts of excuses and subterfuges while he postpones making the explanations which duty and affection urge upon him as necessary for the health and happiness of his child. An unwillingness so strong and irrational as this must have its root in subconscious processes charged with strong feeling.

The tendency to guard children from sexual knowledge and experience seems to be truly universal in civilized man and to surpass all differences of morals, discipline, or taste. Amongst primitive savages the principle has not acquired the altruistic signification which civilized man has given it, but operates as a definite exclusion to be overcome only by solemn ceremonies of initiation and at the price of submission to painful and sometimes mutilating rites.

The constancy of attitude of the adult towards the young, which is thus seen to be so general, evidently gives to the environmental influences which surround the child a fundamental uniformity, and as we have seen, the theory of the development of the individual mind demands that such a uniformity of environmental influence should be shown to be in action.

This is no place to follow out the practical consequences of the fact that every adult necessarily possesses a primary bias in his attitude towards the young, and a bias which is connected with instinctive impulses of great mental energy. However much this tendency is overlaid by moral principles, by altruism, by natural affection, as long as its true nature is unrecognized and excluded from full consciousness its influence upon conduct must be excessive and full of dangerous possibilities. To it must ultimately be traced the scarcely veiled distrust and dislike with which comparative youth is always apt to be met where matters of importance are concerned. The attitude of the adult and elderly towards the enthusiasms of youth is stereotyped in a way which can scarcely fail to strike the psychologist as remarkable and illuminating in its commonplaceness. The youthful revolutionary, who after all is no more essentially absurd than the elderly conservative, is commonly told by the latter that he too at the same age felt the same aspirations, burnt with the same zeal, and yearned with the same hope until he learnt wisdom with experience—" as you will have, my boy, by the time you are my age." To the psychologist the kindly contempt of such pronouncements cannot conceal the pathetic jealousy of declining power. Herd instinct, inevitably siding with the majority and the ruling powers, has always added its influence to the side of age and given a very distinctly perceptible bias to history, proverbial wisdom, and folklore against youth and confidence and enterprise and in favour of age and caution, the immemorial wisdom of the past, and even the toothless mumblings of senile decay.

Any comprehensive survey of modern civilized life cannot fail to yield abundant instances of the disproportionate influence in the conduct of affairs which has been acquired by mere age. When we remember how little in actual practice man proves himself capable of the use of reason, how very little

he actually does profit by experience though the
phrase is always in his mouth, it must be obvious
that there is some strong psychological reason for
the predominance of age, something which must be
determinative in its favour quite apart from its merits
and capacity when competing with youth.   The
" monstrous regiment " of old men—and to the
biologist it is almost as " monstrous " as the
regiment of Mary Stuart was to poor indignant
Knox—extends into every branch of man's activity.
We prefer old judges, old lawyers, old politicians,
old doctors, old generals, and when their functions
involve any immediacy of cause and effect and are
not merely concerned with abstractions, we content-
edly pay the price which the inelasticity of these
ripe minds is sometimes apt to incur.

IV.

If the propositions already laid down prove to be
sound, we must regard the personality of the adult
as the resultant of three groups of forces to which
the mind from infancy onwards is subject ; *first*
the egoistic instincts of the individual pressing for
gratification and possessing the intense mental
energy characteristic of instinctive processes,
secondly the specific sensitiveness to environmental
influences which the mind as that of a gregarious
animal necessarily possesses, a quality capable of
endowing outside influences with the energy of
instinct and, *thirdly* the environmental influences
which act upon the growing mind and are also
essentially determined in their intensity and uniformity by instinctive mechanisms.
The work of Freud has been directed mainly
to the elucidation of the processes included in the
first group—that is to say, to the study of the
primarily egoistic impulses and the modifications

they develop under restraint. He has worked out, in fact, a veritable embryology of the mind.

The embryology of the body is to those who have had no biological training far from being a gratifying subject of contemplation. The stages through which the body passes before reaching its familiar form have a superficial aspect of ugly and repulsive caricature with which only a knowledge of the great compressed pageant of nature they represent can reconcile the mind. The stages through which, according to the doctrines of Freud, the developing mind passes are not less repulsive when judged from the purely human point of view than are the phases of the body which betray its cousinship with the fish and the frog, the lemur and the ape. The works of Nature give no support to the social convention that to be truly respectable one must always have been respectable. All her most elaborate creations have " risen in the world " and are descended in the direct line from creatures of the mud and dust. It is characteristic of her method to work with the humblest materials and to patch and compromise at every step. Any given structure of her making is thus not by any means necessarily the best that could conceivably be contrived, but a workable modification of something else, always more or less conditioned in its functioning by the limitations of the thing from which it was made.

To the biologist, therefore, the fact that Freud's investigations of the development of the mind have shown it passing through stages anything but gratifying to self-esteem will not be either surprising or a ground for disbelief. That Freud's conclusions are decidedly unpalatable when judged by a narrowly human standard is very obvious to any one who is at all familiar with the kind of criticism they have received. It must be acknowledged, moreover, that his methods of exposition have not always tended to disguise the nauseousness of the dose he attempts to administer. Such matters, however, lie altogether apart from the question whether his conclusions are or are not just, though it is perhaps justifiable to say that had these conclusions been immediately acceptable, the fact would be presumptive evidence that they were either not new or were false.

The work of Freud embodies the most determined, thorough, and scientific attempt which has been made to penetrate the mysteries of the mind by the direct human method of approach, making use of intro-spection—guided and guarded, it is true, by an elaborate technique—as its essential instrument. To have shaped so awkward and fallacious an instrument into an apparatus for which accuracy and fruitfulness can be claimed is in itself a notable triumph of psychological skill.

The doctrines of Freud seem to be regarded by his school as covering all the activities of the mind and making a complete, though of course not neces-sarily exhaustive, survey of the whole field. I have already pointed out directions in which it appears to me that inquiries by other methods than those of the psycho-analytic school can be pursued with success. Regarded in a broad way, the Freudian body of doctrine which I have already ventured to describe as essentially an embryology of the mind gives one the impression of being mainly descriptive and systematic rather than dynamic, if one may with due caution use such words. It is able to tell us how such and such a state of affairs has arisen, what is its true significance, and to describe in minute detail the factors into which it can be analysed. When the question of acting upon the mind is raised its resources seem less striking. In this direction its chief activities have been in the treatment of abnormal mental states, and these are dealt with by a laborious process of analysis in which the subject's whole mental development is retraced, and the numerous significant experiences which have become excluded from the conscious field are brought back into it.

When the unconscious processes which underlie the symptoms have been assimilated to the conscious life of the patient, the symptoms necessarily disappear, and the patient's mind gains or regains the " normal " condition. However precious such a cure may be to the patient, and however interesting to the physician, its value to the species has to be judged in relation to the value of the " normal " to which the patient has been restored—that is, in relation to the question as to whether any move, however small, in the direction of an enlargement of the human mind has been made. Until some clearer evidence has been furnished of a capacity for development in this direction the Freudian system should, perhaps, be regarded as more notably a psychology of knowledge than a psychology of power.

It is interesting to notice that in discussing the mechanism of psycho-analysis in liberating the " abnormal " patient from his symptoms, Freud repeatedly lays stress on the fact that the efficient factor in the process is not the actual introduction of the suppressed experiences into the conscious field, but the overcoming of the resistances to such an endeavour. I have attempted to show that these resistances or counter-impulses are of environmental origin, and owe their strength to the specific sensitiveness of the gregarious mind. Resistances of similar type and identical origin are responsible for the formation of the so-called normal type of mind. It is a principal thesis of an earlier essay in this book that this normal type is far from being psychologically healthy, is far from rendering available the full capacity of the mind for foresight and

progress, and being in exclusive command of directing power in the world, is a danger to civilization.
An investigation of the resistant forces that are
encountered by the developing mind is clearly, then,
a matter of the utmost importance. They are now
allowed to come into being haphazard, and while
they undoubtedly contain elements of social value
and necessary restraints, they are the products, not
of a courageous recognition of facts but of fears,
prejudices, and repressed instinctive impulses, and
are consolidated by ignorance, indolence, and tribal
custom.

The interest of the psycho-analytic school has been
turned remarkably little into this field. The speculation may be hazarded that in this direction it might
find the sources of a directer power over the human
mind, and at least some attenuation of that atmosphere of the consulting-room and the mad-house
which does so much to detract from its pretensions
to be a psychological system of universal validity.

Some Principles of a Biological Psychology.

The third method by which it has been attempted
to attack the problems of psychology is that which
I have called the comparative. Its characteristic note
is a distrust of that attitude towards phenomena
which I have called the human point of view.
Man's description and interpretation of his own
mental experience being so liable to distortion by
prejudice, by self-esteem, by his views as to his
own nature and powers, as well as so incomplete by
reason of his incapacity to reach by ordinary introspection the deeper strata of his mind, it becomes
necessary to make action as far as - possible the
subject of observation rather than speech, and to
regard it as a touchstone of motive more important than the actor's own views. The principle

may be exemplified in a simple and concrete form. If a given piece of human behaviour bears the closest resemblance to behaviour which is characteristic of the ape, the sheep, or the wolf, the biologist in attempting to arrive at the actual cause will ascribe an importance to this resemblance at least no less than that he will give to any explanation of the action as rational and deliberate which may be furnished by, the actor or by his own intelligence.

A second principle of the method will be by a study of the whole range of animal life, and especially of forms whose conduct presents obvious resemblances to that of man, to discover what instinctive impulses may be expected to operate in him.

A third principle will be to search for criteria, whereby instinctive impulses or their derivatives arising in the mind can be distinguished from rational motives, or at any rate motives in which the instinctive factor is minimal. Thus will be furnished for the method the objective standard for the judgment of mental observations which is the one indispensable requirement in all psychological inquiries.

When it is known what types of instinctive mechanisms are to be expected, and under what aspects they will appear in the mind, it is possible to press inquiry into many of the obscurer regions of human behaviour and thought, and to arrive at conclusions which, while they are in harmony, with the general body of biological science, have the additional value of being immediately useful in the conduct of affairs.

At the very outset of such researches we are met by an objection which illustrates how different the biological conception of the mind is from that current amongst those whose training has been lite-

rary and philosophic. The objection I am thinking
of is that of the ordinary intellectualist view of
man. According to this we must regard him as
essentially a rational creature, subject, it is true,
to certain feeble relics of instinctive impulsion, but
able to control such without any great expense of
will power, irrational at times in an amiable and
rather " nice " way, but fundamentally always independent, responsible, and captain of his soul. Most
holders of this opinion will of course admit that
in a distant and vague enough past man must have
been much more definitely an instinctive being, but
they regard attempts to trace in modern man any,
considerable residue of instinctive activities as a
tissue of fallacious and superficial analogies, based
upon a shallow materialism and an ignorance of
the great principles of philosophy or a crudeness
which cannot assimilate them.

This objection is an expression of the very
characteristic way in which mankind over-estimates
the practical functioning of reason in his mind and
the influence of civilization on his development. In
an earlier essay I have tried to show to how great
an extent the average educated man is willing to
pronounce decided judgments, all of which he be-
lieves himself to have arrived at by the exercise
of pure reason, upon the innumerable complex
questions of the day. Almost all of them concern
highly technical matters upon none of which has
he the slightest qualification to pronounce. This
characteristic, always obvious enough, has naturally,
during the war shown the exaggeration so apt to
occur in all non-rational processes at a time of
general stress. It is not necessary to catalogue
the various public functions in regard to which
the common citizen finds himself in these days moved
to advise and exhort. They are numerous, and
for the most part highly technical. Generally the

more technical a given matter is, the more vehement and dogmatic is the counsel of the utterly unin- structed counsellor. Even when the questions in- volved are not especially such as can be dealt with only by the expert, the fact that the essential data are withheld from the public by the authorities renders all this amateur statecraft and generalship more than usually ridiculous. Nevertheless, those who find the materials insufficient for dogmatism and feel compelled to a suspense of judgment are apt to fall under suspicion of the crime of failing to " realize " the seriousness of the war. When it is remembered that the duty of the civilian is in no way concerned with these matters of high tech- nique, while he has very important functions to carry out in maintaining the nation's strength if he could be brought to take an interest in them, it seems scarcely possible to argue that such conduct is that of a very highly rational being. In reality the objective examination of man's behaviour, if atten- tion is directed to the facts and not to what the actors think of them, yields at once in every field example after example of similar irrational features.

When the influence of civilization is looked upon as having rendered man's instincts of altogether secondary importance in modern life, it is plain that such a conclusion involves a misconception of the nature of instinct. This well-worn term has come to have so vague a connotation that some definition of it is necessary. The word " instinct " is used here to denote inherited modes of reaction to bodily need or external stimulus. It is difficult to draw a sharp distinction between instinct and mere reflex action, and an attempt to do so with exact precision is of no particular value. In general we may say that the reactions which should be classed under the head of instinct are delayed (that is, not necessarily carried out with fatal promptitude immediately upon the stimulus), complex (that is, consist of acts rather than mere movements), and may be accompanied by quite elaborate mental processes. In a broad way also it may be said that the mental accompaniments of an instinctive process are for the most part matters of feeling. During the growth of the need or stimulus there will be a desire or inclination which may be quite intense, and yet not definitely focused on any object that is consciously realized ; the act itself will be distinguished to the actor by its rightness, obviousness, necessity, or inevitableness, and the sequel of the act will be satisfaction. This mere hint of the psychical manifestations of instinctive activity leaves quite out of account the complex effects which may ensue when two instinctive impulses that have come to be antagonistic reach the mind at the same time. The actual amount of mental activity which accompanies an instinctive process is very variable ; it may be quite small, and then the subject of it is reduced to a mere automaton, possessed, as we say, by an ungovernable passion such as panic, lust, or rage ; it may be quite large, and sometimes the subject, deceived by his own rationalizations and suppressions, may suppose himself to be a fully rational being in undisputed possession of free will and the mastery of his fate at the very moment when he is showing himself to be a mere puppet dancing to the strings which Nature, unimpressed by his valiant airs, relentlessly and impassively pulls.

The extent of the psychical accompaniments of instinctive activity in civilized man should not, therefore, be allowed to obscure the fact that the instincts are tendencies deeply ingrained in the very structure of his being. They are as necessarily inherited, as much a part of himself, and as essential a condition for the survival of himself and his race, as are the vital organs of his body.

Their persistence in him is established and enforced by the effects of millions of years of selection, so that it can scarcely be supposed that a few thousand years of civilized life which have been accompanied by no steady selection against any single instinct can have had any effect whatever in weakening them. The common expression that such an effect has been produced is doubtless due to the great development in civilized man of the mental accompaniments of instinctive processes. These mental phenomena surround the naked reality of the impulse with a cloud of rationalized comment and illusory explanation. The capacity which man possesses for free and rational thought in matters untainted by instinctive inclination is of course indubitable, but he has not realized that there is no obvious mental character attached to propositions having an instinctive basis which should expose them to suspicion. As a matter of fact, it is just those fundamental propositions which owe their origin to instinct which appear to the subject the most obvious, the most axiomatic, and the least liable to doubt by any one but an eccentric or a madman.

It has been customary with certain authors— perhaps especially such as have interested themselves in sociological subjects—to ascribe quite a large number of man's activities to separate instincts. Very little consideration of most of these propositions shows that they are based upon too lax a definition or a want of analysis, for most of the activities referred to special instincts prove to be derivatives of the great primal instincts which are common to or very widely distributed over the animal kingdom. Man and a very large number of all animals inherit the capacity to respond to physical need or emergency according to the demands which we classify as the three primary instincts of self-preservation, nutrition, and reproduction. If a series of animals of increasing brain power be examined, it will be found that a growth of intelligence, while it does nothing to enfeeble the instinctive impulse, modifies the appearances of it by increasing the number of modes of reaction it may use. Intelligence, that is to say, leaves its possessor no less impelled by instinct than his simpler ancestor, but endows him with the capacity to respond in a larger variety of ways. The response is now no longer directly and narrowly confined to a single path, but may follow a number of indirect and intricate ways ; there is no reason, however, to suppose that the impulse is any the weaker for that. To mistake indirectness of response for enfeeblement of impulse is a fundamental error to which all inquiry, into the psychology of instinct is liable.

To man his big brain has given a maximal power of various response which enables him to indulge his instinctive impulses in indirect and symbolic activities to a greater extent than any other animal. It is for this reason that the instincts of man are not always obvious in his conduct and have come to be regarded by some as practically no more than vestigial. Indirect modes of response may indeed become so involved as to assume the appearance of the negation of the very instincts of which they are the expression. Thus it comes to be no paradox to say that monks and nuns, ascetics and martyrs, prove the strength of the great primary instincts their existence seems to deny.

Man and a certain number of other species widely, distributed throughout the animal kingdom show, in addition to the instincts of self-preservation, nutrition, and sex, specialized inherited modes of response to the needs, not directly of the individual but of the herd to which he belongs. These responses, which are perfectly well marked and characteristic, are those of the herd instinct. It is

7

important to grasp clearly the relation of this instinct to the individual. It must be understood that each separate member of a gregarious species inherits characters deeply rooted in his being which effectually differentiate him from any non-gregarious animal. These characters are such that in presence of certain stimuli they will ensure his responding in a specialized way which will be quite different from the response of a solitary animal. The response when examined will be found not necessarily to favour the survival of the individual as such, but to favour his survival as a member of a herd. A very simple example will make this plain. The dog and the cat are our two most familiar examples of the social and the solitary animal respectively. Their different attitudes towards feeding must have been observed by all. The cat takes her food leisurely, without great appearance of appetite and in small amounts at a time ; the dog is voracious and will eat hurriedly as much as he can get, growling anxiously if he is approached. In doing so he is expressing a deeply ingrained characteristic. His attitude towards food was built up when he hunted in packs and to get a share of the common kill had to snatch what came in his way and gulp it down before it could be taken from him. In slang which has a sound biological basis we say he " wolfs " his food. When in domestication his food supply is no longer limited in the primitive way, his instinctive tendency persists ; he is typically greedy and will kill himself by overeating if he is allowed to. Here we have a perfect instance of an instinctive response being disadvantageous to the survival of the individual as such, and favouring his survival only as a member of a herd. This example, trivial as it may seem, is worthy of close study. It shows that the individual of the gregarious species, as an individual and in isolation, possesses indelible marks of character which effectually distinguish him from all solitary animals.

The same principle applies with equal force to man. Whether he is alone or in company, a hermit philosopher or a mere unit of a mob, his responses will bear the same stamp of being regulated by the existence and influence of his fellows.

The foregoing considerations, elementary and incomplete as they are, suggest that there is a strong prima facie case for rejecting the common conceptions that man is among animals the least endowed with an inheritance of instinct, and that civilization has produced in him profound modifications in his primitive instinctive impulses. If the conception which I have put forward be correct, namely, that man is not at all less subject to instinctive impulsions than any other animal but disguises the fact from the observer and from himself by the multiplicity of the lines of response his mental capacity enables him to take, it should follow that his conduct is much less truly variable and much more open to generalization than has generally been supposed. Should this be possible, it would enable the biologist to study the actual affairs of mankind in a really practical way, to analyse the tendencies of social development, to discover how deeply or superficially they were based in the necessity of things, and above all, to foretell their course. Thus might be founded a true science of politics which would be of direct service to the statesman.

Many attempts have been made to apply biological principles to the interpretation of history, and the guidance of statecraft, especially since the popularization of the principles associated with the name of Darwin. Such attempts have generally been undertaken less in the spirit of the scientific

investigator than in that of the politician ; the
point of departure has been a political conviction
and not a biological truth ; and as might be expected,
when there has been any conflict between political
conviction and biological truth it is the latter that
has had to give way. Work of this kind has brought
the method into deserved contempt by its crudity,
its obvious subservience to prejudice, and its pre-
tentious gestures of the doctrinaire. England has
not been without her examples of these scientific
politicians and historians, but they cannot be said
to have flourished here as they have in the more
scholastic air of Germany. The names of several
such are now notorious in this country and their
works are sufficiently familiar for it to be obvious
that their claims to scientific value do not admit of
discussion.   It is not necessary to consider their
conclusions, they are condemned by their manner ;
and however interesting their political vociferation
may be to fellow-patriots, it plainly has no meaning
whatsoever as science.   In face of the spectacle
presented by these leather-lunged doctrinaires, it
needs some little hardihood to maintain that it is
possible profitably to apply biological principle to
the consideration of human affairs ; nevertheless, that
is an essential thesis of this essay.

In attempting to illuminate the records of history
by the principles of biology, an essential difficulty is
the difference of scale in time upon which these
two departments of knowledge work.   Historical
events are confined within a few thousands of years,
the biological record covers many millions ; it is
scarcely to be expected, therefore, that even a gross
movement on the cramped historical scale will be
capable of detection in the vast gulf of time the
biological series represents. A minor difficulty is
the fact that the data of history come to us through
a dense and reduplicated veil of human interpre-

tation, whereas the biological facts are comparatively free from this kind of obscuration. The former obstacle is undoubtedly serious. It is to be remarked, however, that there is strong reason to suppose that the process of organic evolution has not been and is not always infinitely slow and gradual. It is more than suspected that, perhaps as the result of slowly accumulated tendency or perhaps as the result of a sudden variation of structure or capacity, there have been periods of rapid change which might have been perceptible to direct observation. The infinitely long road still tending upwards comes to where it branches and meets another path, tending perhaps downwards or even upwards at a different slope. May not the meeting or branching form, as it were, a node in the infinite line, a resting place for the eye, a point in the vast extension capable of recognition by a finite mind and of expression in terms of human affairs? It is the belief of the writer that the human race stands at such a nodal point to-day.

THE BIOLOGY OF GREGARIOUSNESS.

In order to set forth the evidence on which is based the conclusion that the present juncture of affairs is not merely, as it very obviously is, a meeting-place of epochs in the historical series, but also marks a stage in the biological series which will prove to have been a moment of destiny in the evolution of the human species, it will be necessary to inquire somewhat closely into the biological meaning of the social habit in animals. In an earlier essay certain speculations in the same subject were indulged, and a certain amount of repetition will be necessary. The point of view then taken up, however, was different from that from which I shall now attempt to review the facts. Then the main interest lay in an examination of the meaning of gregariousness for the individual mind, and although reasons enough were found for uneasiness at the course of events, and at the instability of civilization which any radical examination displayed, the inquiry was not pursued under any immediate imminence of disaster to the social fabric as it must be now. Naturally, therefore, at the present time certain aspects of the subject which before were of no special relevance become of great importance and demand close examination.

In a general view of the social habit in animals certain outstanding facts are readily to be observed. It is of wide distribution and sporadic occurrence, it varies much in the completeness of its development, and there seems to be an inverse relation between its completeness and the brain power of the animal concerned.

From the wideness of its distribution the social habit may be supposed to represent a forward step in complexity which comes about readily. It has the appearance of being upon a path which species have a natural tendency to follow, a line of evolution which is perhaps rendered possible by constantly occurring small variations common to all animals and taken advantage of only under certain circumstances of pressure or increase. It seems not to depend on any sudden large variation of type, and such is not necessary to account for it. It differs from many other modifications which we know animal life to have undergone in being immediately useful to the species from its very beginning and in its least perfect forms. Once started, however imperfectly, the new habit will have a natural tendency to progress towards fuller forms of sociality by reason of special selective forces which it inevitably sets going. The fact that it is valuable to the species in which it develops even in its most larval forms, combined with its tendency to progress, no doubt accounts for the wonderful series of all degrees of gregariousness which the field of natural history presents.

I have pointed out elsewhere that the fundamental biological meaning of gregariousness is that it allows of an indefinite enlargement of the unit upon which the undifferentiated influence of natural selection is allowed to act, so that the individual merged in the larger unit is shielded from the immediate effects of natural selection and is exposed directly only to the special form of selection which obtains within the new unit.

There seems little doubt that this sheltering of the individual allows him to vary and to undergo modifications with a freedom which would have been dangerous to him as an isolated being, but is safe under the new conditions and valuable to the new unit of which he now is a part.

In essence the significance of the passage from the solitary to the gregarious seems to be closely similar to that of the passage from the unicellular to the multicellular organism—an enlargement of the unit exposed to natural selection, a shielding of the individual cell from that pressure, an endowment of it with freedom to vary and specialize in safety.

Nature has thus made two great experiments of the same type, and if one be reasonably careful to avoid arguing from analogy, it is possible to use one case to illuminate the other by furnishing hints as to what mechanisms may be looked for and in what directions inquiry may profitably be pursued.

The sporadic occurrence of gregariousness at widely separated points of the animal field—in man and sheep, in ant and elephant—inclines one to suppose that multicellularity must have arisen also at multiple points, and that the metazoa did not arise from the protozoa by a single line of descent. It suggests also that there is some inherent property in mobile living organisms that makes combination of individuals into larger units a more or less inevitable course of development under certain circumstances and without any gross variation being necessary to initiate it. The complex evolution which multicellularity made possible, and perhaps enforced, can scarcely fail to make one wonder whether the gregarious animal has not entered upon a path which must of necessity lead to increasing complexity and co-ordination, to a more and more stringent intensity of integration or to extinction.

The varying degrees to which the social habit has developed among different animals provide a very interesting branch of study. The class of insects is remarkable in furnishing an almost inexhaustible variety of stages to which the instinct is developed. Of these that reached by the humble bee, with its small, weak families, is a familiar example of a low grade ; that of the wasp, with its colonies large and strong, but unable to survive the winter, is another of more developed type ; while that of the honey bee represents a very high grade of development in which the instinct seems to have completed its cycle and yielded to the hive the maximum advantages of which it is capable. In the honey bee, then, the social instinct may be said to be complete.

It is necessary to examine somewhat closely into what is denoted by the completeness or otherwise of the social habit in a given species.

To return for a moment to the case of the change from the unicellular to the multicellular, it is obvious that in the new unit, to get the full advantage of the change there must be specialization involving both loss and gain to the individual cell ; one loses power of digestion and gains a special sensitiveness to stimulation, another loses locomotion to gain digestion, and so forth in innumerable series as the new unit becomes more complex. Inherent, however, in the new mechanism is the need for co-ordination if the advantages of specialization are to be obtained. The necessity of a nervous system— if progress is to be maintained—early becomes obvious, and it is equally clear that the primary function of the nervous system is to facilitate co-ordination. Thus it would seem that the individual cell incorporated in a larger unit must possess a capacity for specialization, the ability to originate new methods of activity, and a capacity for response —that is, the ability to limit itself to action co-ordinated suitably to the interests of the new unit rather than to those that would have been its own if it had been a free unit in itself. Specialization and co-ordination will be the two necessary conditions for success of the larger unit, and advance in complexity will be possible as long only as these two are unexhausted. Neither, of course, will be of avail without the other. The richest specialization will be of no good if it cannot be controlled to the uses of the whole organism, and the most perfect control of the individual cells will be incapable of ensuring progress if it has no material of original variation to work on.

The analogy is helpful in the consideration of the mechanisms brought into play by the social habit. The community of the honey bee bears a close resemblance to the body of a complex animal. The capacity for actual structural specialization of the individuals in the interests of the hive has been remarkable and has gone far, while at the same time co-ordination has been stringently enforced, so that each individual is actually absorbed into the community, expends all its activities therein, and when excluded from it is almost as helpless as a part of the naked flesh of an animal detached from its body. The hive may, in fact, without any very undue stretch of fantasy, be described as an animal of which all the individual cells have retained the power of locomotion. When one watches the flight of a swarm of bees its unanimity and directness very easily produce the illusion that one is witnessing the migration of a single animal usually sedentary but at times capable of undertaking journeys with a formidable and successful energy. This new animal differs from the other animals of the metazoa which it has outdistanced in the race of evolution, not merely in its immense power, energy, and flexibility, but also in the almost startling fact that it has recovered the gift of immortality which seemed to have been lost with its protozoal ancestors.

The extent to which the hive makes use of the powers of its individuals is the measure of the completeness with which the social habit is developed in it. The worker bee has practically no activities which are not directly devoted to the hive, and yet she goes about her ceaseless tasks in a way that never fails to impress the observer with its exuberant energy and even its appearance of joyfulness. It is thought that the average worker bee *works herself to death* in about two months. That is a fact which can scarcely fail to arouse, even in the least imaginative, at any rate a moment of profound contemplation.

If we could suppose her to be conscious in the human sense, we must imagine the bee to be possessed by an enthusiasm for the hive more intense than a mother's devotion to her son, without personal ambitions, or doubts or fears, and if we are to judge by the imperfect experience man has yet had of the same lofty passion, we must think of her consciousness, insignificant spark as it is, as a little fire ablaze with altruistic feeling. Doubtless, such an attribution of emotion to the bee is a quite unjustified fallacy of anthropomorphism. Nevertheless, it is not altogether valueless as a hint of what social unity might effect in an animal of larger mental life. There can be little doubt that the perfection to which the communal life of the bee has attained is dependent on the very smallness of the mental development of which the individuals are capable. Their capacity to assimilate experience is necessarily from their structure, and is known by experience to be, small and their path is marked out so plainly by actual physical modifications that the almost miraculous absorption of the worker in the hive is after all perhaps natural enough. If she were able to assimilate general experience on a larger scale, to react freely and appropriately to stimuli external to the hive, there can be little doubt that the community would show a less concentrated efficiency than it does to-day. The standing miracle of the bee—her sensitiveness to the voice of the hive and her capacity to communicate with her fellows—would undoubtedly be less marvellously perfect if she were not at the same time deaf to all other voices.

When we come to consider animals in which the anatomist can recognize a brain and the psychologist an individual mind, the types of gregariousness we meet with are found to have lost the magnificent intensity of the bee. This decline in intensity seems to be due to the greatly increased variety of reaction of which the individual is capable. The gregarious mammalia are most of them relatively intelligent, they are capable of assimilating experience to a certain extent and have a definite capacity for individual existence. In them the social habit shows comparatively little tendency to a gradual intensification, but is a more static condition. Doubtless, there are other conditions which also limit it. For example, the slowness of multiplication and fixity of structure in the mammalia obviously deprive them of the possibility of undergoing a continuous social integration as the insects have. Be this as it may, we find in them the social habit but little or scarcely at all expressed in physical specialization but shown as a deeply ingrained mental character which profoundly influences their habits and their modes of reaction to bodily and external impressions. Among the mammalia other than man and possibly apes and monkeys, gregariousness is found in two broadly distinguishable types according to the function it subserves. It may be either protective as in the sheep, the deer, the ox, and the horse, or aggressive as in the wolf and allied animals. In both forms it will involve certain common types of capacity, while the distinguishing characteristic of each will be a special kind of reaction to certain stimuli. It is important to understand that these peculiarities are possessed by each individual of the larger unit, and will be displayed by him in a characteristic way whether he is in the company of his fellows or not. It is not necessary to repeat here in any detail the characters of the gregarious mammal. They have been dealt with in an earlier essay, but it is desirable to emphasize here certain features of exceptional importance and some which were but little discussed before.

The quite fundamental characteristic of the social mammal, as of the bee, is sensitiveness to the voice of his fellows. He must have the capacity to react fatally and without hesitation to an impression coming to him from the herd, and he must react in a totally different way to impressions coming to him from without. In the presence of danger his first motion must be, not to fly or to attack as the case may be, but to notify the herd. This characteristic is beautifully demonstrated in the low growl a dog will give at the approach of a stranger. This is obviously in no way part of the dog's programme of attack upon his enemy—when his object is intimidation he bursts into barking—but his first duty is to put the pack on its guard. Similarly the start of the sheep is a notification and precedes any motion of flight.

In order that the individual shall be sensitive in a special degree to the voice of the herd, he must have developed in him an infallible capacity for recognizing his fellow-members. In the lower mammalia this seems almost exclusively a function of the sense of smell, as is natural enough since that sense is as a general rule highly developed in them. The domestic dog shows admirably the importance of the function of recognition in his species. Comparatively few recognize even their masters at any distance by sight or sound, while obviously with their fellows they are practically dependent on smell. The extent to which the ceremonial of recognition has developed in the dog is, of course, very familiar to every one. It shows unmistakable evidence of the rudiments of social organization, and is not the less illuminating to the student of human society for having a bodily orientation and technique which at first sight obscures its resemblance to similar, and it is supposed more dignified, mechanisms in man.

Specialization fitting the animal for social life is obviously in certain directions restrictive ; that is, it denies him certain capacities and immunities which the solitary animal possesses ; equally obviously is it in certain directions expansive and does it confer qualities on the social which the solitary does not possess. Among qualities of restrictive specialization are inability to live satisfactorily apart from the herd or some substitute for it, the liability to loneliness, a dependence on leadership, custom, and tradition, a credulity towards the dogmas of the herd and an unbelief towards external experience, a standard of conduct no longer determined by personal needs but influenced by a power outside the ego—a conscience, in fact, and a sense of sin—a weakness of personal initiative and a distrust of its promptings. Expansive specialization, on the other hand, gives the gregarious animal the sense of power and security in the herd, the capacity to respond to the call of the herd with a maximum output of energy and endurance, a deep-seated mental satisfaction in unity with the herd, and a solution in it of personal doubts and fears.

All these characters can be traced in an animal such as the dog. The mere statement of them, necessarily in mental terms, involves the liability to a certain inexactitude if it is not recognized that no hypothesis as to the consciousness of the dog is assumed but that the description in mental terms is given because of its convenient brevity. An objective description of the actual conduct on which such summarized statements are founded would be impossibly voluminous.

The advantage the new unit obtains by aggressive gregariousness is chiefly its immense accession of strength as a hunting and fighting organism. Protective gregariousness confers on the flock or herd advantages perhaps less obvious but certainly not less important. A very valuable gain is the increased efficiency of vigilance which is possible. Such efficiency depends on the available number of actual watchers and the exquisite sensitiveness of the herd and all its members to the signals of such sentries. No one can have watched a herd of sheep for long without being impressed with the delicacy with which a supposed danger is detected, transmitted throughout the herd, and met

by an appropriate movement.   Another advantage
enjoyed by the new unit is a practical solution of
the difficulties incident upon the emotion of fear.
Fear is essentially an enfeebling passion, yet in the
sheep and such animals it is necessarily developed
to a high degree in the interests of safety.   The
danger of this specialization is neutralized by the
implication of so large a part of the individual's
personality, in the herd and outside of himself.
Alarm becomes a passion, as it were, of the herd
rather than of the individual, and the appropriate
response by the individual is to an impulse received
from the herd and not directly from the actual
object of alarm.   It seems to be in this way that the
paralysing emotion of fear is held back from the
individual, while its effect can reach him only as the
active and formidable passion of panic.   The
gregarious herbivora are in fact timid but not fearful
animals.   All the various mechanisms in which the
social habit shows itself apparently have as their
general function a maximal sensitiveness to danger
of the herd as a whole, combined with maintaining
with as little interruption as possible an atmosphere
of calm within the herd, so that the individual
members can occupy themselves in the serious
business of grazing.   It must be doubted whether
a truly herbivorous animal of a solitary habit could
ever flourish when we remember how incessant must
be his industry in feeding if he is to be properly
nourished, and how much such an occupation will
be interfered with by the constant alarms he must be
subject to if he is to escape the attacks of carnivorous
enemies.   The evidence suggests that protective gregariousness is a more elaborate manifestation of
the social habit than the aggressive form.   It is
clear that the security of the higher herbivora, such
as the ox and especially the horse and their allies, is
considerable in relation to the carnivora.   One may

permissibly perhaps indulge the speculation that in the absence of man the horse possibly might have developed a greater complexity of organization than it has actually been able to attain ; that the facts should seem to contain this hint is a curious testimony to the wonderful constructive imagination of Swift.

Setting aside such guesses and confining ourselves to the facts, we may say in summary that we find the infrahuman mammalia to present two distinctly separable strains of the social habit. Both are of great value to the species in which they appear, and both are associated with certain fundamentally similar types of reactive capacity which give a general resemblance of character to all gregarious animals. Of the two forms the protective is perhaps capable of absorbing more fully the personality of the individual than is the aggressive, but both seem to have reached the limit of their intensification at a grade far lower than that which has been attained in the insects.

Characters of the Gregarious Animal displayed by Man.

When we come to consider man we find ourselves faced at once by some of the most interesting problems in the biology of the social habit. It is probably not necessary now to labour the proof of the fact that man is a gregarious animal in literal fact, that he is as essentially gregarious as the bee and the ant, the sheep, the ox, and the horse. The tissue of characteristically gregarious reactions which his conduct presents furnishes incontestable proof of this thesis, which is thus an indispensable clue to an inquiry into the intricate problems of human society.

It is desirable perhaps to enumerate in a summary

way the more obvious gregarious characters which man displays.

1. He is intolerant and fearful of solitude, physical or mental. This intolerance is the cause of the mental fixity and intellectual incuriousness which, to a remarkable degree for an animal with so capacious a brain, he constantly displays. As is well known, the resistance to a new idea is always primarily a matter of prejudice, the development of intellectual objections, just or otherwise, being a secondary process in spite of the common delusion to the contrary. This intimate dependence on the herd is traceable not merely in matters physical and intellectual, but also betrays itself in the deepest recesses of personality as a sense of incompleteness which compels the individual to reach out towards some larger existence than his own, some encompassing being in whom his perplexities may find a solution and his longings peace. Physical loneliness and intellectual isolation are effectually solaced by the nearness and agreement of the herd. The deeper personal necessities cannot be met—at any rate, in such society as has so far been evolved—by, so superficial a union ; the capacity for intercommunication is still too feebly developed to bring the individual into complete and soul-satisfying harmony with his fellows, to convey from one to another

> Thoughts hardly to be packed
> Into a narrow act,
> Fancies that broke through language and escaped.

Religious feeling is therefore a character inherent in the very structure of the human mind, and is the expression of a need which must be recognized by the biologist as neither superficial nor transitory. It must be admitted that some philosophers and

8

men of science have at times denied to the religious impulses of man their true dignity and importance. Impelled perhaps by a desire to close the circle of a materialistic conception of the universe, they, have tended to belittle the significance of such phenomena as they were unable to reconcile with their principles and bring within the iron circle of their doctrine. To deal with religion in this way has not only been an outrage upon true scientific method, but has always led to a strong reaction in general opinion against any radical inquiry by science into the deeper problems of man's nature and status. A large and energetic reaction of this kind prevails to-day. There can be little doubt that it was precipitated, if not provoked, by attempts to force a harsh and dogmatic materialism into the status of a general philosophy. As long as such a system is compelled to ignore, to depreciate, or to deny the reality of such manifestly important phenomena as the altruistic emotions, the religious needs and feelings, the experiences of awe and wonder and beauty, the illumination of the mystic, the rapture of the prophet, the unconquerable endurance of the martyr, so long must it fail in its claims to universality. It is therefore necessary to lay down with the strongest emphasis the proposition that the religious needs and feelings of man are a direct and necessary manifestation of the inheritance of instinct with which he is born, and therefore deserve consideration as respectful and observation as minute as any other biological phenomenon.

2. He is more sensitive to the voice of the herd than to any other influence. It can inhibit or stimulate his thought and conduct. It is the source of his moral codes, of the sanctions of his ethics and philosophy. It can endow him with energy, courage, and endurance, and can as easily take these away.

It can make him acquiese in his own punishment
and embrace his executioner, submit to poverty,
bow to tyranny, and sink without complaint under
starvation.   Not merely can it make him accept
hardship and suffering unresistingly, but it can make
him accept as truth the explanation that his perfectly
preventable afflictions are sublimely just and gentle.
It is in this acme of the power of herd suggestion
that is perhaps the most absolutely incontestable
proof of the profoundly gregarious nature of man.
That a creature of strong appetites and luxurious
desires should come to tolerate uncomplainingly his
empty belly, his chattering teeth, his naked limbs,
and his hard bed is miracle enough.   What are we
to say of a force which, when he is told by the full-
fed and well-warmed that his state is the more
blessed can make him answer, " How beautiful I
How true I "   In the face of so effectual a negation,
not merely of experience and common sense but also
of actual hunger and privation, it is not possible to
set any limits to the power of the herd over the
individual.

3. He is subject to the passions of the pack in
his mob violence and the passions of the herd in
his panics.   These activities are by no means limited
to the outbursts of actual crowds, but are to be
seen equally clearly in the hue and cry of newspapers and public after some notorious criminal or
scapegoat, and in the success of scaremongering by
the same agencies.

4. He is remarkably susceptible to leadership.
This quality in man may very naturally be thought
to have a basis essentially rational rather than instinctive if its manifestations are not regarded with
a special effort to attain an objective attitude.   How
thoroughly reasonable it appears that a body of men
seeking a common object should put themselves
under the guidance of some strong and expert

personality who can point out the path most profitably to be pursued, who can hearten his followers
and bring all their various powers into a harmonious
pursuit of the common object. The rational basis
of the relation is, however, seen to be at any rate
open to discussion when we consider the qualities
in a leader upon which his authority so often rests,
for there can be little doubt that their appeal is
more generally to instinct than to reason. In ordinary politics it must be admitted that the gift of
public speaking is of more decisive value than anything else. If a man is fluent, dextrous, and ready
on the platform, he possesses the one indispensable
requisite for statesmanship ; if in addition he has
the gift of moving deeply the emotions of his hearers,
his capacity for guiding the infinite complexities
of national life becomes undeniable. Experience
has shown that no exceptional degree of any other
capacity is necessary to make a successful leader.
There need be no specially arduous training, no great
weight of knowledge either of affairs or the human
heart, no receptiveness to new ideas, no outlook
into reality. Indeed, the mere absence of such seems
to be an advantage ; for originality is apt to appear
to the people as flightiness, scepticism as feebleness, caution as doubt of the great political principles
that may happen at the moment to be immutable.
The successful shepherd thinks like his sheep, and
can lead his flock only if he keeps no more than the
shortest distance in advance. He must remain, in
fact, recognizable as one of the flock, magnified
no doubt, louder, coarser, above all with more urgent
wants and ways of expression than the common
sheep, but in essence to their feeling of the same
flesh with them. In the human herd the necessity
of the leader bearing unmistakable marks of identification is equally essential. Variations from the
normal standard in intellectual matters are tolerated

if they are not very conspicuous, for man has never yet taken reason very seriously, and can still look upon intellectuality as not more than a peccadillo if it is not paraded conspicuously ; variations from the moral standard are, however, of a much greater significance as marks of identification, and when they become obvious, can at once change a great and successful leader into a stranger and an outcast, however little they may seem to be relevant to the adequate execution of his public work. If a leader's marks of identity with the herd are of the right kind, the more they are paraded the better. We like to see photographs of him nursing his little grand-daughter, we like to know that he plays golf badly, and rides the bicycle like our common selves, we enjoy hearing of " pretty incidents " in which he has given the blind crossing-sweeper a penny or begged a glass of water at a wayside cottage—and there are excellent biological reasons for our gratification.

In times of war leadership is not less obviously based on instinct, though naturally, since the herd is exposed to a special series of stresses, manifestations of it are also somewhat special. A people at war feels the need of direction much more intensely than a people at peace, and as always they want some one who appeals to their instinctive feeling of being directed, comparatively regardless of whether he is able in fact to direct. This instinctive feeling inclines them to the choice of a man who presents at any rate the appearance and manners of authority and power rather than to one who possesses the substance of capacity but is denied the shadow. They have their conventional pictures of the desired type—the strong, silent, relentless, the bold, outspoken, hard, and energetic—but at all costs he must be a " man," a " leader who can lead," a shepherd, in fact, who, by his gesticulations and his shouts, leaves his flock in no doubt as to his presence and his activity. It is touching to remember how often a people in pursuit of this ideal has obtained and accepted in response to its prayers nothing but melodramatic bombast, impatience, rashness, and foolish, boasting truculence ; and to remember how often a great statesman in his country's need has had to contend not merely with her foreign enemies, but with those at home whose vociferous malignity has declared his magnanimous composure to be sluggishness, his cautious scepticism to be feebleness, and his unostentatious resolution to be stupidity.

5. His relations with his fellows are dependent upon the recognition of him as a member of the herd. It is important to the success of a gregarious species that individuals should be able to move freely within the large unit while strangers are excluded. Mechanisms to secure such personal recognition are therefore a characteristic feature of the social habit. The primitive olfactory greeting common to so many of the lower animals was doubtless rendered impossible for man by his comparative loss of the sense of smell long before it ceased to accord with his pretensions, yet in a thriving active species the function of recognition was as necessary as ever. Recognition by vision could be of only limited value, and it seems probable that speech very early became the accepted medium. Possibly the necessity to distinguish friend from foe was one of the conditions which favoured the development of articulate speech. Be this as it may, speech at the present time retains strong evidence of the survival in it of the function of herd recognition. As is usual with instinctive activities in man, the actual state of affairs is concealed by a deposit of rationalized explanation which is apt to discourage merely superficial inquiry. The function of conversation is, it is to be supposed, ordinarily regarded

as being the exchange of ideas and information.
Doubtless it has come to have such a function, but
an objective examination of ordinary conversation
shows that the actual conveyance of ideas takes
a very small part in it. As a rule the exchange
seems to consist of ideas which are necessarily
common to the two speakers, and are known to
be so by each. The process, however, is none
the less satisfactory for this ; indeed, it seems even
to derive its satisfactoriness therefrom. The inter-
change of the conventional lead and return is
obviously very far from being tedious or meaningless to the interlocutors. They can, however, have
derived nothing from it but the confirmation to one
another of their sympathy and of the class or classes
to which they belong.

Conversations of greeting are naturally particularly rich in the exchange of purely ceremonial
remarks, ostensibly based on some subject like the
weather, in which there must necessarily be an
absolute community of knowledge. It is possible,
however, for a long conversation to be made up
entirely of similar elements, and to contain no trace
of any conveyance of new ideas ; such intercourse
is probably that which on the whole is most satisfactory to the " normal " man and leaves him more
comfortably stimulated than would originality or
brilliance, or any other manifestation of the strange
and therefore of the disreputable.

Conversation between persons unknown to one
another is also—when satisfactory—apt to be rich
in the ritual of recognition. When one hears or
takes part in these elaborate evolutions, gingerly
proffering one after another of one's marks of
identity, one's views on the weather, on fresh air
and draughts, on the Government and on uric acid,
watching intently for the first low hint of a growl,
which will show one belongs to the wrong pack

and must withdraw, it is impossible not to be reminded of the similar manœuvres of the dog, and to be thankful that Nature has provided us with a less direct, though perhaps a more tedious, code.

It may appear that we have been dealing here with a far-fetched and laboured analogy, and making much of a comparison of trivialities merely for the sake of compromising, if that could be done, human pretensions to reason. To show that the marvel of human communion began, perhaps, as a very humble function, and yet retains traces of its origin, is in no way to minimize the value or dignity of the more fully developed power. The capacity for free intercommunication between individuals of the species has meant so much in the evolution of man, and will certainly come in the future to mean so incalculably more, that it cannot be regarded as anything less than a master element in the shaping of his destiny.

Some Peculiarities of the Social Habit in Man.

It is apparent after very little consideration that the extent of man's individual mental development is a factor which has produced many novel characters in his manifestations of the social habit, and has even concealed to a great extent the profound influence this instinct has in regulating his conduct, his thought, and his society.

Large mental capacity in the individual, as we have already seen, has the effect of providing a wide freedom of response to instinctive impulses, so that, while the individual is no less impelled by instinct than a more primitive type, the manifestations of these impulses in his conduct are very varied, and his conduct loses the appearance of a narrow concentration on its instinctive object. It needs only to pursue this reasoning to a further stage to reach the conclusion that mental capacity, while in no way limiting the impulsive power of instinct, may, by providing an infinite number of channels into which the impulse is free to flow, actually prevent the impulse from attaining the goal of its normal object. In the ascetic the sex instinct is defeated, in the martyr that of self-preservation, not because these instincts have been abolished, but because the activity of the mind has found new channels for them to flow in. As might be expected, the much more labile herd instinct has been still more subject to this deflection and dissipation without its potential impulsive strength being in any way impaired. It is this process which has enabled primitive psychology so largely to ignore the fact that man still is, as much as ever, endowed with a heritage of instinct and incessantly subject to its influence. Man's mental capacity, again, has enabled him as a species to flourish enormously, and thereby to increase to a prodigious extent the size of the unit in which the individual is merged. The nation, if the term be used to describe every organization under a completely independent, supreme government, must be regarded as the smallest unit on which natural selection now unrestrictedly acts. Between such units there is free competition, and the ultimate regulator of these relations is physical force. This statement needs the qualification that the delimitation between two given units may be much sharper than that between two others, so that in the first case the resort to force is likely to occur readily, while in the second case it will be brought about only by the very ultimate necessity. The tendency to the enlargement of the social unit has been going on with certain temporary relapses throughout human history.

Though repeatedly, checked by the instability of the larger units, it has always resumed its activity, so that it should probably be regarded as a fundamental biological drift the existence of which is a factor which must always be taken into account in dealing with the structure of human society.

The gregarious mind shows certain characteristics which throw some light on this phenomenon of the progressively enlarging unit. The gregarious animal is different from the solitary in the capacity to become conscious in a special way, of the existence of other creatures. This specific consciousness of his fellows carries with it a characteristic element of communion with them. The individual knows another individual of the same herd as a partaker in an entity of which he himself is a part, so that the second individual is in some way, and to a certain extent identical with himself and part of his own personality. He is able to feel with the other and share his pleasures and sufferings as if they, were an attenuated form of his own personal experiences. The degree to which this assimilation of the interests of another person is carried depends, in a general way, on the extent of the intercommunication between the two. In human society, a man's interest in his fellows is distributed about him concentrically, according to a compound of various relations they, bear to him which we may call in a broad way their nearness. The centrifugal fading of interest is seen when we compare the man's feeling towards one near to him with his feeling towards one farther off. He will be disposed, other things being equal, to sympathize with a relative as against a fellow-townsman, with a fellow-townsman as against a mere inhabitant of the same county, with the latter as against the rest of the country, with an Englishman as against a European, with a European as against an Asiatic, and so on until a limit is reached beyond which all human interest is lost. The distribution of interest is of course never purely geographical, but is modified by, for example, trade and professional sympathy, and by special cases of intercommunication which bring topographically distant individuals into a closer grade of feeling than their mere situation would demand. The essential principle, however, is that the degree of sympathy with a given individual varies directly with the amount of intercommunication with him. The capacity to assimilate the interests of another individual with one's own, to allow him, as it were, to partake in one's own personality, is what is called altruism, and might equally well perhaps be called expansive egoism. It is a characteristic of the gregarious animal, and is a perfectly normal and necessary development in him of his instinctive inheritance.

Altruism is a quality the understanding of which has been much obscured by its being regarded from the purely human point of view. Judged from this standpoint, it has been apt to appear as a breach in the supposedly "immutable" laws of "Nature red in tooth and claw," as a virtue breathed into man from some extra-human source, or as a weakness which must be stamped out of any race which is to be strong, expanding, and masterful. To the biologist these views are equally false, superfluous, and romantic. He is aware that altruism occurs only in a medium specifically protected from the unqualified influence of natural selection, that it is the direct outcome of instinct, and that it is a source of strength because it is a source of union.

In recent times, freedom of travel, and the development of the resources rendered available by education, have increased the general mass of intercommunication to an enormous extent. Side by side with this, altruism has come more and more into recognition as a supreme moral law. There is already a strong tendency to accept selfishness as a test of sin, and consideration for others as a test of virtue, and this has influenced even those who by public profession are compelled to maintain that right and wrong are to be defined only in terms of an arbitrary extra-natural code.

Throughout the incalculable ages of man's existence as a social animal, Nature has been hinting to him in less and less ambiguous terms that altruism must become the ultimate sanction of his moral code. Her whispers have never gained more than grudging and reluctant notice from the common man, and from those intensified forms of the common man, his pastors and masters. Only to the alert senses of moral genius has the message been at all intelligible, and when it has been interpreted to the people it has always been received with obloquy and derision, with persecution and martyrdom. Thus, as so often happens in human society, has one manifestation of herd instinct been met and opposed by another.

As intercommunication tends constantly to widen the field of action of altruism, a point is reached when the individual becomes capable of some kind of sympathy, however attenuated, with beings outside the limits of the biological unit within which the primitive function of altruism lies. This extension is perhaps possible only in man. In a creature like the bee the rigidly limited mental capacity of the individual and the closely organized society of the hive combine to make the boundary of the hive correspond closely with the uttermost limit of the field over which altruism is active. The bee, capable of great sympathy and understanding in regard to her fellow-members of the hive, is utterly callous and without understanding in regard to any creature of external origin and existence. Man, however, with his infinitely greater capacity for assimilating experience, has not been able to maintain the rigid limitation of sympathy to the unit, the boundaries of which tend to acquire a certain indefiniteness not seen in any of the lower gregarious types.

Hence tends to appear a sense of international justice, a vague feeling of being responsibly concerned in all human affairs and by a natural consequence the ideas and impulses denoted under the term " pacifism."

One of the most natural and obvious consequences of war is a hardening of the boundaries of the social unit and a retraction of the vague feelings towards international sympathy which are a characteristic product of peace and intercommunication. Thus it comes about that pacifism and internationalism are in great disgrace at the present time ; they are regarded as the vapourings of cranky windbags who have inevitably been punctured at the first touch of the sword ; they are, our political philosophers tell us, but products of the miasm of sentimental fallacy which tends to be bred in the relaxing atmosphere of peace. Perhaps no general expressions have been more common since the beginning of the war, in the mouths of those who have undertaken our instruction in the meaning of events, than the propositions that pacifism is now finally exploded and shown always to have been nonsense, that war is and always will be an inevitable necessity in human affairs as man is what is called a fighting animal, and that not only is the abolition of war an impossibility, but should the abolition of it unhappily prove to be possible after all and be accomplished, the result could only be degeneration and disaster.

Biological considerations would seem to suggest that these generalizations contain a large element of inexactitude. The doctrine of pacifism is a perfectly natural development, and ultimately inevitable in an animal having an unlimited appetite for experience and an indestructible inheritance of social instinct. Like all moral discoveries made in the haphazard, one-sided way which the lack of co-ordination in human society forces upon its moral pioneers, it has necessarily an appearance of crankiness, of sentimentality, of an inaptitude for the grasp of reality. This is normal and does not in the least affect the value of the truth it contains. Legal and religious torture were doubtless first attacked by cranks ; slavery was abolished by them. Advocacy by such types does not therefore constitute an argument of any weight against their doctrines, which can adequately be judged only by some purely objective standard. Judged by such a standard, pacifism, as we have seen, appears to be a natural development, and is directed towards a goal which unless man's nature undergoes a radical change will probably be attained. That its attainment has so far been foreseen only by a class of men possessing more than the usual impracticability of the minor prophet is hardly to be considered a relevant fact.

It is impossible to leave this subject without some comment on the famous doctrine that war is a biological necessity. Even if one knew nothing of those who have enunciated this proposition, its character would enable one to suspect it of being the utterance of a soldier rather than a biologist. There is about it a confidence that the vital effects of war are simple and easy to define and a cheerful contempt for the considerable biological difficulties of the subject that remind one of the bracing military atmosphere, in which a word of command is the supreme fact, rather than that of the laboratory, where facts are the masters of all. It may be supposed that even in the country of its birth the doctrine seemed more transcendently true in times of peace amid a proud and brilliant regime than it does now after more than twelve months of war. The whole conception is of a type to arouse interest in its psychological origin rather than in a serious discussion of its merits. It arose in a military State abounding in prosperity and progress of very recent growth, and based upon three short wars which had come closely one after another and formed an ascending series of brilliant success. In such circumstances even grosser assumptions might very well flourish and some such doctrine was a perfectly natural product. The situation of the warrior-biologist was in some way that of the orthodox expounder of ethics or political economy —his conclusions were ready-made for him; all he had to do was to find the "reasons" for them. War and war only had produced the best and greatest and strongest State—indeed, the only State worthy of the name; therefore war is the great creative and sustaining force of States, or the universe is a mere meaningless jumble of accidents. If only wars would always conform to the original Prussian pattern, as they did in the golden age from 1864 to 1870—the unready adversary, the few pleasantly strenuous weeks or months, the thumping indemnity! That is the sort of biological necessity one can understand. But twelve months of agonizing, indecisive effort in Poland and Russia and France, might have made the syllogism a little less perfect, the new law of Nature not quite so absolute.

These matters, however, are quite apart from the practical question whether war is a necessity to maintain the efficiency and energy of nations and to prevent them sinking into sloth and degeneracy. The problem may be stated in another form. When we take a comprehensive survey of the natural history of man—using that term to include the whole of his capacities, activities, and needs, physical, intellectual, moral—do we find that war is the indispensable instrument whereby his survival and progress as a species are maintained? We are assuming in this statement that progress or increased elaboration is to continue to be a necessary tendency in his course by which his fate, through the action of inherited needs, powers, and weaknesses, and of external pressure is irrevocably conditioned. The assumption, though commonly made, is by no means obviously true. Some of the evidence justifying it will be dealt with later ; it will not be necessary here to do more than note that we are for the moment treating the doctrine of human progress as a postulate.

Man is unique among gregarious animals in the size of the major unit upon which natural selection and its supposedly chief instrument, war, is open to act unchecked. There is no other animal in which the size of the unit, however laxly held together, has reached anything even remotely approaching the inclusion of one-fifth or one-quarter of the whole species. It is plain that a mortal contest between two units of such a monstrous size introduces an altogether new mechanism into the hypothetical " struggle for existence " on which the conception of the biological necessity of war is founded. It is clear that that doctrine, if it is to claim validity, must contemplate at any rate the possibility of a war of extremity, even of something like extermination, which shall implicate perhaps a third of the whole human race. There is no parallel in biology for progress being accomplished as the result of a racial impoverishment so extreme, even if it were accompanied by a closely specific

selection instead of a mere indiscriminate destruction. Progress is undoubtedly dependent mainly
on the material that is available for selection being
rich and varied. Any great reduction in the amount
and variety of what is to be regarded as the raw
material of elaboration necessarily must have as
an infallible effect, the arrest of progress. It may be
objected, however, that anything approaching extermination could obviously not be possible in a war
between such immense units as those of modern man.
Nevertheless, the object of each of the two adversaries would be to impose its will on the other, and to
destroy in it all that was especially individual, all
the types of activity and capacity which were the
most characteristic in its civilization and therefore
the cause of hostility. The effect of success in such
an endeavour would be an enormous impoverishment
of the variety of the race and a corresponding effect
on progress.

To this line of speculation it may perhaps further
be objected that the question is not of the necessity
of war to the race as a whole, but to the individual
nation or major unit. The argument has been used
that when a nation is obviously the repository of
all the highest gifts and tendencies of civilization,
the race must in the end benefit, if this nation, by
force if necessary, imposes its will and its principles
on as much of the world as it can. To the biologist
the weakness of this proposition—apart from the
plain impossibility of a nation attaining an objective
estimate of the value of its own civilization—is that
it embodies a course of action which tends to the
spread of uniformity and to limit that variety of
material which is the fundamental quality essential
for progress. In certain cases of very gross discrepancy between the value of two civilizations, it
is quite possible that the destruction of the simpler
by the more elaborate does not result in any great

9

loss to the race through the suppression of valuable varieties.   Even this admission is, however,
open to debate, and it may well be doubted whether
in some ways the wholesale extermination of " inferior " races has not denied to the species the
perpetuation of lines of variation which might have
been of great value.

It seems remarkable that among gregarious
animals other than man direct conflict between major
units such as can lead to the suppression of the less
powerful is an inconspicuous phenomenon.   They
are, it may be supposed, too busily engaged in maintaining themselves against external enemies to have
any opportunities for fighting within the species.
Man's complete conquest of the grosser enemies of
his race has allowed him leisure for turning his
restless pugnacity—a quality no longer fully occupied upon his non-human environment—against his
own species.   When the major units of humanity
were small the results of such conflict were not
perhaps very serious to the race as a whole, except
in prolonging the twilight stages of civilization.   It
can scarcely be questioned that the organization
of a people for war tends to encourage unduly a
type of individual who is abnormally insensitive to
doubt, to curiosity, and to the development of original
thought.   With the enlargement of the unit and the
accompanying increase in knowledge and resources,
war becomes much more seriously expensive to the
race.   In the present war the immense size of the
units engaged and their comparative equality in
power have furnished a complete *reductio ad ab-
surdum* of the proposition that war in itself is
a good thing even for the individual nation.   It
would seem, then, that in the original proposition
the word " war " must be qualified to mean a war
against a smaller and notably weaker adversary.
The German Empire was founded on such wars.

The conception of the biological necessity, of war,
may fairly, be expected to demonstrate its validity
in the fate of that Empire, if such a demonstration
is ever to be possible. Every condition for a crucial
experiment was present : a brilliant inauguration in
the very atmosphere of military, triumph, a conscious
realization of the value of the martial spirit, a determination to keep the warrior ideal conspicuously,
foremost with a people singularly able and willing
to accept it. If this is the way in which an ultimate world-power is to be founded and maintained,
no single necessary, factor is lacking. And yet
after a few years, in what should be the very, first
youth of an Empire, we find it engaged against
a combination of Powers of fabulous strength, which,
by a miracle of diplomacy, no one else could have
accomplished, it has united against itself. It is
an irrelevance to assert that this combination is the
result of malice, envy, treachery, barbarism,; such
terms are by hypothesis not admissible. If the
system of Empire-building is not proof against those
very elementary, enemies, any further examination
of it is of course purely academic. To withstand
those is just what the Empire is there for ; if it
falls a victim to them, it fails in its first and simplest
function and displays a radical defect in its structure.,
To the objectivist practice is the only test in human
affairs, and he will not allow his attention to be
distracted from what did happen by, the most perfectly logical demonstration of what ought to have
happened. It is the business of an Empire not to
encounter overwhelming enemies. Declaring itself
to be the most perfect example of its kind and
the foreordained heir of the world will remain no
more than a pleasant—and dangerous—indulgence,
and will not prevent it showing by, its fate that
the fruits of perfection and the promise of permanence are not demonstrated in the wholesale

manufacture of enemies and in the combination of them into an alliance of unparalleled strength.

The doctrine of the biological necessity of war may, then, be regarded as open to strong suspicion on theoretical grounds of being contrary to the evolutionary tendency already plainly marked out for the human species. The fact that the nation in which its truth was most generally accepted has been led—and undoubtedly to some extent by it —into a war which can scarcely fail to prove disastrous suggests that in the practical field it is equally fallacious. It may well, therefore, be removed to the lumber-room of speculation and stored among the other pseudo-scientific dogmas of political " biologists "—the facile doctrines of degeneracy, the pragmatic lecturings on national characteristics, on Teutons and Celts, on Latins and Slavs, on pure races and mixed races, and all the other ethnological conceits with which the ignorant have gulled the innocent so long.

IMPERFECTIONS OF THE SOCIAL HABIT IN MAN.

The study of man as a gregarious animal has not been pursued with the thoroughness and objectivity it deserves and must receive if it is to yield its full value in illuminating his status and in the managenent of society. The explanation of this comparative neglect is to be found in the complex irregularity which obscures the social habit as manifested by man. Thus it comes to be believed that gregariousness is no longer a fully functional and indispensable inheritance, but survives at the present day merely in a vestigial form as an interesting but quite unimportant relic of primitive activities. We have already shown that man is ruled by instinctive impulses just as imperative and just as

characteristically social as those of any other gregarious animal.   A further argument that he is
to-day as actively and essentially a social animal
as ever is furnished by the fact that he suffers
from the disadvantages of such an animal to a
more marked degree perhaps than any other.   In
physical matters he owes to his gregariousness and
its uncontrolled tendency to the formation of crowded
communities with enclosed dwellings, the seriousness of many of his worst diseases, such as tuber-
culosis, typhus, and plague ; there is no evidence
that these diseases effect anything but an absolutely
indiscriminate destruction, killing the strong and
the weakly, the socially useful and the socially useless, with equal readiness, so that they cannot be
regarded as even of the least selective value to
man.   The only other animal which is well known
to suffer seriously from disease as a direct consequence of its social habit is the honey bee—as
has been demonstrated by recent epidemics of
exterminating severity.

In mental affairs, as I have tried to show, man
owes to the social habit his inveterate resistiveness
to new ideas, his submission to tradition and pre-
cedent, and the very serious fact that governing
power in his communities tends to pass into the hands
of what I have called the stable-minded—a class
the members of which are characteristically insensitive to experience, closed to the entry of new
ideas, and obsessed with the satisfactoriness of things
as they are.   At the time when this corollary of
gregariousness was first pointed out—some ten years
ago—it was noted as a serious flaw in the stability
of civilization. The suggestion was made that as
long as the great expert tasks of government necessarily gravitated into the hands of a class which
characteristically lacked the greater developments of
mental capacity and efficiency, the course of civiliza-

tion must continue to be at the mercy of accident and disaster. The present European war—doubtless in the actual state of affairs a remedy no less necessary because of its dreadfulness—is an example on the greatest possible scale of the kind of price the race has to pay for the way in which minds and temperaments are selected by its society.

When we see the great and serious drawbacks which gregariousness has entailed on man, it cannot but be supposed that that course of evolution has been imposed upon him by a real and deep-seated peculiarity of his nature—a fatal inheritance which it is impossible for him to repudiate.

When we inquire why it is that the manifestations of gregariousness in man are so ambiguous that their biological significance has been to a great extent overlooked, the answer seems to be furnished by that capacity for various reaction which is the result of his general mental development, and which has tended almost equally to obscure his other instinctive activities. It may be repeated once more that in a creature such as the bee the narrow mental capacity of the individual limits reaction to a few and relatively simple courses, so that the dominance of instinct in the species can to the attentive observer never be long in doubt. In man the equal dominance of instinct is obscured by the kaleidoscopic variety of the reactions by which it is more or less effectually satisfied.

While to a superficial examination of society the evidences of man's gregarious inheritance are ambiguous and trivial, to the closer scrutiny of the biologist it soon becomes obvious that in society, as constituted to-day the advantageous mechanisms rendered available by that inheritance are not being made use of to anything approaching their full possibilities. To such an extent is this the case that the situation of man as a species even is probably a good deal more precarious than has usually been supposed by those who have come to be in charge of its destinies. The species is irrevocably committed to a certain evolutionary path by the inheritance of instinct it possesses. This course brings with it inevitable and serious disadvantages as well as enormously greater potential advantages. As long as the spirit of the race is content to be submissive to the former and indifferent to the discovery and development of the latter, it can scarcely have a bare certainty of survival and much less of progressive enlargement of its powers.

In the society of the bee two leading characteristics are evident—an elaborate and exact specialization of the individual, and a perfect absorption of the interests of the individual in those of the hive;; these qualities seem to be the source of the unique energy and power of the whole unit and of the remarkable superiority of intelligence it possesses over the individual member. It is a commonplace of human affairs that combined action is almost invariably less intelligent than individual action, a fact which shows how very little the members of the species are yet capable of combination and co-ordination and how far inferior—on account, no doubt, of his greater mental capacity,—man is in this respect to the bee.

This combination of specialization and moral homogeneity should be evident in human society, if it is taking advantage of its biological resources. Both are, in fact, rather conspicuously absent.

There is abundant specialization of a sort; but it is inexact, lax, wasteful of energy, and often quite useless through being on the one hand superfluous or on the other incomplete. We have large numbers of experts in the various branches of science

and the arts, but we insist upon their adding to
the practice of their specialisms the difficult task
of earning their living in an open competitive
market.   The result is that we tend to get at the
summit of our professions only those rare geniuses
who combine real specialist capacity with the arts
of the bagman.   An enormous proportion of our
experts have to earn their living by teaching—an
exhausting and exacting art for which they are not
at all necessarily qualified, and one which demands
a great amount of time for the earning of a very,
exiguous pittance.

The teaching of our best schools, a task so
important that it should be entrusted to none but
those highly qualified by nature and instruction in
the art, is almost entirely in the hands of athletes and
grammarians of dead languages.   We choose as
our governors amateurs of whom we demand fluency,
invincible prejudice, and a resolute blindness to dissentient opinion.   In commerce we allow ourselves
to be overrun by a multitude of small and mostly,
inefficient traders struggling to make a living by
the supply of goods from the narrow and ageing
stocks which are all they can afford to keep.   We
allow the supply of our foodstuffs to be largely
in the hands of those who cannot afford to be clean,
and submit out of mere indifference to being fed
on meat, bread, vegetables which have been for an
indefinite period at the mercy of dirty middlemen,
the dust and mud and flies of the street, and the
light-hearted thumbing errand-boy.   We allow a
large proportion of our skilled workers to waste
skill and energy on the manufacture of things which
are neither useful nor beautiful, on elaborate
specialist valeting, cooking, gardening for those
who are their inferiors in social activity, and
value.

The moral homogeneity so plainly, visible in the

society of the bee is replaced in man by a segregation into classes which tends always to obscure the unity of the nation and often is directly antagonistic to it. The readiness with which such segregation occurs seems to be due to the invincible strength of the gregarious impulse in the individual man and to the immense size and strength of the modern major unit of the species. It would appear that in order that a given unit should develop the highest degree of homogeneity within itself it must be subject to direct pressure from without. A great abundance of food supply and consequent relaxed external pressure may in the bee lead to indiscriminate swarming, while in man the size and security of the modern State lead to a relaxation of the closer grades of national unity—in the absence of deliberate encouragement of it or of the stimulus of war. The need of the individual for homogeneity is none the less present, and the result is segregation into classes which form, as it were, minor herds in which homogeneity is maintained by the external pressure of competition, of political or religious differences and so forth. Naturally enough such segregations have come to correspond in a rough way with the various types of imperfect specialization which exist. This tendency is clearly of unfavourable effect on national unity, since it tends to obscure the national value of specialization and to give it a merely local and class significance. Segregation in itself is always dangerous in that it provides the individual with a substitute for the true major unit—the nation—and in times when there is an urgent need for national homogeneity may prove to be a hostile force.

It has been characteristic of the governing classes to acquiesce in the fullest developments of segregation and even to defend them by force and to fail to realize in times of emergency, that national

homogeneity must always be a partial and weakly
passion as long as segregation actively persists.

Class segregation has thus come to be regarded
as a necessary and inevitable part of the structure
of society. Telling as it does much more in the
favour of certain classes than others, it has come to
be defended by a whole series of legal and moral
principles invented for the purpose, and by arguments that to objective examination are no more
than rationalized prejudice. The maintenance of
the social system—that is, of the segregation of
power and prestige, of ease and leisure, and the
corresponding segregations of labour, privation, and
poverty,—depends upon an enormously elaborate
system of rationalization, tradition, and morals, and
upon almost innumerable indirect mechanisms
ranging from the drugging of society with alcohol
to the distortion of religious principle in the interests
of the established order. To the biologist the whole
immensely intricate system is a means for combating
the slow, almost imperceptible, pressure of Nature
in the direction of a true national homogeneity.
That this must be attained if human progress is to
continue is, and has long been, obvious. The further
fact that it can be attained only by a radical change
in the whole human attitude towards society is but
barely emerging from obscurity.

The fact that even the immense external stimulus
of a great war now fails to overcome the embattled
forces of social segregation, and can bring about
only a very partial kind of national homogeneity in
a society where segregation is deeply ingrained,
seems to show that simple gregariousness has run its
course in man and has been defeated of its full
maturity by the disruptive power of man's capacity
for varied reaction. No state of equilibrium can be
reached in a gregarious society short of complete

homogeneity, so that, failing the emergence of some new resource of Nature, it might be suspected that man, as a species, has already begun to decline from his meridian. Such a new principle is the conscious direction of society by man, the refusal by him to submit indefinitely to the dissipation of his energies and the disappointment of his ideals in inco-ordination and confusion. Thus would appear a function for that individual mental capacity of man which has so far, when limited to local and personal ends, tended but to increase the social confusion.

A step of evolution such as this would have consequences as momentous as the first appearance of the multicellular or of the gregarious animal. Man, conscious as a species of his true status and destiny, realizing the direction of the path to which he is irrevocably committed by Nature, with a moral code based on the unshakable natural foundation of altruism, could begin to draw on those stores of power which will be opened to him by a true combination, and the rendering available in co-ordinated action of the maximal energy of each individual.

GREGARIOUS SPECIES AT WAR.

The occurrence of war between nations renders obvious certain manifestations of the social instinct which are apt to escape notice at other times. So marked is this that a certain faint interest in the biology of gregariousness has been aroused during the present war, and has led to some speculation but no very radical examination of the facts or explanation of their meaning. Expression, of course, has been found for the usual view that primitive instincts normally vestigial or dormant are aroused into activity by the stress of war, and that there is a process of rejuvenation of " lower " instincts at the expense of " higher." All such views, apart from their theoretical unsoundness, are uninteresting because they are of no practical value.

It will be convenient to mention some of the more obvious psychological phenomena of a state of war before dealing with the underlying instinctive processes which produce them.

The war that began in August 1914 was of a kind peculiarly suitable to produce the most marked and typical psychological effects. It had long been foreseen as no more than a mere possibility of immense disaster—of disaster so outrageous that by that very fact it had come to be regarded with a passionate incredulity. It had loomed before the people, at any rate of England, as an event almost equivalent to the ultimate overthrow of all things. It had been led up to by years of doubt and anxiety, sometimes rising to apprehension, sometimes lapsing into unbelief, and culminating in an agonized period of suspense, while the avalanche tottered and muttered on its base before the final and still incredible catastrophe. Such were the circumstances which no doubt led to the actual outbreak producing a remarkable series of typical psychological reactions.

The first feeling of the ordinary citizen was fear— an immense, vague, aching anxiety, perhaps typically vague and unfocused, but naturally tending soon to localize itself in channels customary to the individual and leading to fears for his future, his food supply, his family, his trade, and so forth. Side by side with fear there was a heightening of the normal intolerance of isolation. Loneliness became an urgently unpleasant feeling, and the individual experienced an intense and active desire for the company and even physical contact of his fellows. In such company he was aware of a great accession of confidence, courage, and moral power. It was possible for an observant person to trace the actual influence of his circumstances upon his judgment, and to notice that isolation tended to depress his confidence while company fortified it. The necessity for companionship was strong enough to break down the distinctions of class, and dissipate the reserve between strangers which is to some extent a concomitant mechanism. The change in the customary frigid atmosphere of the railway train, the omnibus, and all such meeting-places was a most interesting experience to the psychologist, and he could scarcely fail to be struck by its obvious biological meaning.° Perhaps the most striking of all these early phenomena was the strength and vitality of rumour, probably because it afforded by far the most startling evidence that some other and stronger force than reason was at work in the formation of opinion. It was, of course, in no sense an unusual fact that non-rational opinion should be so widespread ; the new feature was that such opinion should be able to spread so rapidly and become established so firmly altogether regardless of the limits within which a given opinion tends to remain localized in times of peace. Non-rational opinion under normal conditions is as a rule limited in its extent by a very strict kind of segregation ; the successful rumours of the early periods of the war invaded all classes and showed a capacity to overcome prejudice, education, or scepticism. The observer, clearly conscious as he might be of the mechanisms at work, found himself irresistibly drawn to the acceptance of the more popular beliefs ; and even the most convinced believer in the normal prevalence of non-rational belief could scarcely have exaggerated the actual state of affairs. Closely allied with this accessibility to rumour was the readiness with which suspicions of treachery and active hostility grew and flourished about any one of even foreign appearance or origin. It is not intended to attempt to discuss the origin and meaning of the various types of fable which have been epidemic in opinion ; the fact we are concerned with here is their immense vitality and power of growth.

We may now turn to some consideration of the psychological significance of these phenomena of a state of war.

The characteristic feature of a really dangerous national struggle for existence is the intensity of the stimulus it applies to the social instinct. It is not that it arouses " dormant " or decayed instincts, but simply that it applies maximal stimulation to instinctive mechanisms which are more or less constantly in action in normal times. In most of his reactions as a gregarious animal in times of peace, man is acting as a member of one or another class upon which the stimulus acts. War acts upon him as a member of the greater herd, the nation, or, in other words, the true major unit. As I have repeatedly pointed out, the cardinal mental character-istic of the gregarious animal is his sensitiveness to his fellow-members of the herd. Without them his personality is, so to say, incomplete ; only in rela-tion to them can he attain satisfaction and personal stability. Corresponding with his dependence on them is his openness towards them, his specific accessibility to stimuli coming from the herd.

A threat directed towards the whole herd is the intensest stimulus to these potentialities, and the individual reacts towards it in the most vigorous way.[1] The first response is a thrill of alarm which

---

[1] War in itself is by no means necessarily a maximal stimulus to herd instinct if it does not involve a definite threat to the whole herd. This fact is well shown in the course of the South African War of 1899–1901. This war was not and was not regarded as capable of becoming a direct threat to the life of the nation. There was con-sequently no marked moral concentration of the people, no massive energizing of the Government by a homogeneous nation, and therefore

passes through the herd from one member to another with magic rapidity. It puts him on the alert, sets him looking for guidance, prepares him to receive commands, but above all draws him to the herd in the first instinctive concentration against the enemy. In the presence of this stimulus even such partial and temporary isolation as was possible without it becomes intolerable. The physical presence of the herd, the actual contact and recognition of its members, becomes indispensable. This is no mere functionless desire, for re-embodiment in the herd at once fortifies courage and fills the individual with moral power, enthusiasm, and fortitude. The meaning that mere physical contact with his fellows still has for man is conclusively shown in the use that has been made of attacks in close formation in the German armies. It is perfectly clear that a densely crowded formation has psychological advantages in the face of danger, which enable quite ordinary beings to perform what are in fact prodigies of valour. Even undisciplined civil mobs have, on occasion, proved wonderfully valorous, though their absence of unity, often causes their enterprise to alternate with panic. A disciplined mob—if one may use that word merely as a physical expression, without any derogatory meaning—has been shown in this war on innumerable occasions to be capable of facing dangers the facing of which by isolated individuals would be feats of fabulous bravery.

the conduct of the war was in general languid, timid, and pessimistic. The morale of the people was as a whole bad; there was an exaggerated hunger for good news, and an excessive satisfaction in it; an exaggerated pessimism was excited by bad news, and public fortitude was shaken by casualties which we should now regard as insignificant. Correspondingly the activity and vitality of rumour were enormously less than they have been in the present war. The weaker stimulus is betrayed throughout the whole series of events by the weakness of all the characteristic gregarious responses.

The psychological significance of the enormous activity of rumour in this war is fairly plain. That rumours spread readily and are tenacious of life is evidence of the sensitiveness to herd opinion which is so characteristic of the social instinct. The gravity of a threat to the herd is shown by nothing better than by the activity of rumour. The strong stimulus to herd instinct produces the characteristic response in the individual of a maximal sensitiveness to his fellows—to their presence or absence, their alarms and braveries, and in no less degree to their opinions. With the establishment of this state of mind the spread and survival of rumours become inevitable, and will vary directly with the seriousness of the external danger. Into the actual genesis of the individual rumours and the meaning of their tendency to take a stereotyped form we cannot enter here.

The potency of rumour in bearing down rational scepticism displays unmistakably the importance of the instinctive processes on which it rests. It is also one of the many evidences that homogeneity within the herd is a deeply rooted necessity for gregarious animals and is elaborately provided for by characteristics of the gregarious mind.

The establishment of homogeneity in the herd is the basis of morale. From homogeneity proceed moral power, enthusiasm, courage, endurance, enterprise, and all the virtues of the warrior. The peace of mind, happiness, and energy of the soldier come from his feeling himself to be a member in a body solidly united for a single purpose. The impulse towards unity that was so pronounced and universal at the beginning of the war was, then, a true and sound instinctive movement of defence. It was prepared to sacrifice all social distinctions and local prejudices if it could liberate by doing so Nature's inexhaustible stores of moral power for the defence of the herd. Naturally enough its significance was misunderstood, and a great deal of its beneficent magic was wasted by the good intentions which man is so touchingly ready to accept as a substitute for knowledge. Even the functional value of unity was, and still is, for the most part ignored. We are told to weariness that the great objection to disunion is that it encourages the enemy. According to this view, apparent disunion is as serious as real ; whereas it must be perfectly obvious that anything which leads our enemy to under-estimate our strength, as does the belief that we are disunited when we are not, is of much more service to us than is neutralized by any more or less visionary disservice we do ourselves by fortifying his morale. The morale of a nation at war proceeds from within itself, and the mere pharisaism and conceit that come from the contemplation of another's misfortunes are of no moral value. Modern civilians in general are much too self-conscious to conduct the grave tragedy of war with the high, preoccupied composure it demands. They are apt to think too much of what sort of a figure they are making before the world, to waste energy in superfluous explanations of themselves, in flustered and voluble attempts to make friends with bystanders, in posing to the enemy, and imagining they can seriously influence him by grimaces and gesticulations. As a matter of fact, it must be confessed that if such manœuvres could be conducted with a deliberate and purposeful levity which few would now have the fortitude to employ, there would be a certain satisfaction to be obtained in this particular war by the knowledge of our adversary conscientiously, perhaps a little heavily, and with immense resources of learning " investigating our psychology " upon materials of a wholly fantastic kind. Such a design, however, is very far from being the intention of our interpreters to the world, and as long as they cannot keep the earnest and hysterical note out of their exposition it were much better for us that they were totally dumb.

To the psychologist it is plain that the seriousness of disunion is the discouragement to ourselves it necessarily involves. In this lies its single and its immense importance. Every note of disunion is a loss of moral power of incalculable influence; every, evidence of union is an equally incalculable gain of moral power. Both halves of this statement deserve consideration, but the latter is incomparably the more important. If disunion were the more potent influence, a great deal might be done for national morale by the forcible control of opinion and expression. That, however, could yield nothing positive, and we must rely upon voluntary unity, as the only source of all the higher developments of moral power.

It was towards this object that we dimly groped when we felt in the early weeks of the war the impulses of friendliness, tolerance, and goodwill towards our fellow-citizens, and the readiness to sacrifice what privileges the social system had endowed us with in order to enjoy the power which a perfect homogeneity of the herd would have given us.

A very small amount of conscious, authoritative direction at that time, a very little actual sacrifice of privilege at that psychological moment, a series of small, carefully selected concessions none of which need have been actually subversive of prescriptive right, a slight relaxation in the vast inhumanity of the social machine would have given the needed readjustment out of which a true national homogeneity would necessarily have grown.

The psychological moment was allowed to pass, and the country, was spared the shock of seeing its

moral strength, which should of course be left to
luck, fortified by the hand of science. The history
of England during the first fourteen months of the
war was thus left to pursue its characteristically
English course. The social system of class segregation soon repented of its momentary softness and
resumed its customary rigidity. More than that,
it decided that, far from the war being a special
occasion which should penetrate with a transforming
influence the whole of society, from top to bottom,
as the common people were at first inclined to
think, the proper pose before the enemy was to be
that it made no difference at all. We were to continue imperturbably with the conduct of our business,
and to awe the Continent with a supreme exhibition
of British phlegm. The national consciousness of
the working-man was to be stimulated by his
continuing to supply us with our dividends, and
ours by continuing to receive them. It is not
necessary to pursue the history of this new substitute
for unity. It is open to doubt whether our enemies
were greatly appalled by the spectacle, or more so
than our friends ; it is certain that the stimulant supplied to the working-man proved to be inadequate
and had to be supplemented by others. . . .

The problem of the function of the common
citizen in war was of course left unsolved. It was
accepted that if a man were unfit for service and
not a skilled worker, he himself was a mere dead
weight, and his intense longing for direct service,
of however humble a kind, a by-product of which
the State could make no use.

That the working classes have to a certain extent
failed to develop a complete sense of national unity
is obvious enough. It is contended here that what
would have been easy in the early days of the war
and actually inexpensive to prescriptive right, has
steadily become more and more costly to effect

and less and less efficiently done. We are already faced with the possibility of having to make profound changes in the social system to convince the working-man effectually that his interests and ours in this war are one.

That a very large class of common citizens, incapable of direct military work, has been left morally derelict during all these agonizing months of war has probably not been any less serious a fact, although the recognition of it has not been forced unavoidably on public notice. It must surely be clear that in a nation engaged in an urgent struggle for existence, the presence of a large class who are as sensitive as any to the call of the herd, and yet cannot respond in any active way, contains very grave possibilities. The only response to that relentless calling that can give peace is in service ; if that be denied, restlessness, uneasiness, and anxiety must necessarily follow. To such a mental state are very easily added impatience, discontent, exaggerated fears, pessimism, and irritability. It must be remembered that large numbers of such individuals were persons of importance in peace time and retain a great deal of their prestige under the social system we have decided to maintain, although in war time they are obviously without function. This group of idle and flustered parasites has formed a nucleus from which have proceeded some of the many outbursts of disunion which have done so much to prevent this country from developing her resources with smoothness and continuity. It is not suggested that these eruptions of discontent are due to any kind of disloyalty ; they are the result of defective morale, and bear all the evidences of coming from persons whose instinctive response to the call of the herd has been frustrated and who, therefore, lack the strength and composure of those whose souls are uplifted by a satisfactory instinctive activity. Moral instability has been characteristic of all the phenomena of disunion we are now considering, such as recrudescences of political animus, attacks on individual members of the Government, outbursts of spy mania, campaigns of incitement against aliens and of blustering about reprisals. Similar though less conspicuous manifestations are the delighted circulation of rumours, the wild scandalmongering, the eager dissemination of pessimistic inventions which are the pleasure of the smaller amongst these moral waifs. Of all the evidences of defective morale, however, undoubtedly the most general has yet to be mentioned, and that is the proffering of technical advice and exhortation. If we are to judge by what we read, there are few more urgent temptations than this, and yet it is easy to see that there are few enterprises which demand a more complete abrogation of reason. It is almost always the case that the subject of advice is one upon which all detailed knowledge is withheld by the authorities. This restriction of materials, however, seems generally to be regarded by the volunteer critic as giving him greater scope and freedom rather than as a reason for silence or even modesty.

It is interesting to notice in this connection what those who have the ear of the public have conceived to be their duty towards the nation and to try to estimate its value from the point of view of morale. It is clear that they have in general very rightly understood that one of their prime functions should be to keep the Government working in the interests of the nation to the fullest stretch of its energy and resources. Criticism is another function, and advice and instruction a third which have also been regarded as important.

The third of these activities is, no doubt, that which has been most abused and is least important.

It tends on the one hand to get involved in technical military matters and consequent absurdity, and on the other hand, in civil matters, to fall back into the bad old ways of politics. Criticism is obviously a perfectly legitimate function, and one of value as long as it keeps to the field of civil questions, and can free itself of the moral failure of being acrimonious in tone. In a government machine engaged upon the largest of tasks there will always be enough injustice and inhumanity, fraud and foolishness to keep temperate critics beneficially employed.

It is in the matter of stimulating the energy and resolution of the Government that the psychologist might perhaps differ to some extent from the popular guides of opinion. In getting work out of a living organism it is necessary to determine what is the most efficient stimulus. One can make a man's muscles contract by stimulating them with an electric battery, but one can never get so energetic a contraction with however strong a current as can be got by the natural stimulus sent out from the man's brain. Rising to a more complex level, we find that a man does not do work by order so well or so thoroughly as he does work that he desires to do voluntarily. The best way to get our work done is to get the worker to want to do it. The most urgent and potent of all stimuli, then, are those that come from within the man's soul. It is plain, therefore, that the best way to extract the maximum amount of work from members of a Government—and it is to yield this, at whatever cost to themselves, that they are there—is not by the use of threats and objurgations, by talk of impeachment or dismissal, or by hints of a day of reckoning after the war, but by keeping their souls full of a burning passion of service. Such a supply of mental energy can issue only from a

truly homogeneous herd, and it is therefore tō the
production of such a homogeneity of feeling that
we come once more as the one unmistakable
responsibility of the civilian.

We have seen reason to believe that there was
a comparatively favourable opportunity of establishing such a national unity in the early phases of
the war, and that the attainment of the same result
at this late period is likely to be less easy and more
costly of disturbance to the social structure.

The simplest basis of unity is equality, and this
has been an important factor in the unity which in
the past has produced the classically successful manifestations of moral and military power, as for example
in the cases of Puritan England and Revolutionary
France. Such equality as obtained in these cases
was doubtless chiefly moral rather than material,
and it can scarcely be questioned that equality of
consideration and of fundamental moral estimation
is a far more efficient factor than would be equality
of material possessions. The fact that it is difficult
to persuade a man with thirty shillings a week that
he has as much to lose by the loss of national
independence as a man with thirty thousand a year,
is merely evidence that the imagination of the former
is somewhat restricted by his type of education,
and that we habitually attach an absurd moral significance to material advantages. It seems certain
that it would still be possible to attain a very fair
approximation to a real moral equality without any
necessary disturbance of the extreme degree of
material inequality which our elaborate class segregation has imposed upon us.

A serious and practical attempt to secure a true
moral unity of the nation would render necessary,
a general understanding that the state to be striven
for was something different, not only in degree
but also in quality, from anything which has yet

been regarded as satisfactory. A mere intellectual unanimity in the need for prosecuting the war with all vigour, we may be said actually to possess, but its moral value is not very great. A state of mind directed more to the nation and less immediately to the war is what is needed ; the good soldier absorbed in his regiment has little inclination to concern himself with the way the war is going, and the civilian should be similarly absorbed in the nation. To attain this he must feel that he belongs to the country and to his fellow-citizens, and that it and they also belong to him. The established social system sets itself steadily to deny these propositions, and not so much by its abounding material inequalities as by the moral inequalities that correspond with them. The hierarchies of rank, prestige, and consideration, at all times showing serious inconsistencies with functional value, and in war doing so more than ever, are denials of the essential propositions of perfect citizenship, not, curiously enough, through their arbitrary distribution of wealth, comfort, and leisure, but through their persistent, assured, and even unconscious assumption that there exists a graduation of moral values equally real and, to men of inferior station, equally arbitrary. To a gregarious species at war the only tolerable claim to any kind of superiority must be based on leadership. Any other affectation of superiority, whether it be based on prescriptive right, on tradition, on custom, on wealth, on birth, or on mere age, arrogance, or fussiness, and not on real functional value to the State, is, however much a matter of course it may seem, however blandly it may be asserted or picturesquely displayed, an obstacle to true national unity.

Psychological considerations thus appear to indicate a very plain duty for a large class of civilians who have complained of and suffered patriotically

from the fact that the Government has found nothing
for them to do. Let all those of superior and
assured station make it a point of honour and duty
to abrogate the privileges of consideration and
prestige with which they are arbitrarily endowed.
Let them persuade the common man that they also
are, in the face of national necessity, common men.
The searching test of war has shown that a proportion of the population, serious enough in mere
numbers, but doubly serious in view of its power
and influence, has led an existence which may fairly
be described as in some degree parasitic. That
is to say, what they have drawn from the common
stock in wealth and prestige has been immensely
larger than what they have contributed of useful
activity in return. Now, in time of war, they have
still less to give proportionally to what they have
received. Their deplorably good bargain was in
no way of their making ; no one has the slightest
right to attack their honour or good faith ; they
are as patriotically minded as any class, and have
contributed their fighting men to the Army as gener-
ously as the day labourer and the tradesman. It
is therefore not altogether impossible that they might
come to understand the immense opportunity that
is given them by fate to promote a true, deep,
and irresistibly potent national unity.

A further contribution to the establishment of
a national unity of this truly Utopian degree might
come from a changed attitude of mind towards his
fellows in the individual. There would have to
be an increased kindliness, generosity, patience, and
tolerance in all his relations with others, a deliberate attempt to conquer prejudice, irritability,
impatience, and self-assertiveness, a deliberate encouragement of cheerfulness, composure, and fortitude. All these would be tasks for the individual

to carry out for himself alone ; there would be no campaign-making, no direct exhortation, no appeals. Towards the Army and the Navy the central fact of each man's attitude would be the question, " Am I worth dying for ? " and his strongest effort would be the attempt to make himself so.

That question may perhaps make one wonder why it has not been heard more often during the war as a text of the Church. There is little doubt that very many men whose feeling towards the Church is in no way disrespectful or hostile are conscious of a certain uneasiness in hearing her vigorously defending the prosecution of the war and demonstrating its righteousness. They feel, in spite of however conclusive demonstrations to the contrary, that there is a deep-seated inconsistency, between war for whatever object and the Sermon on the Mount, and they cannot but remember, when they are told that this is a holy war, that that also the Germans say. They perhaps feel that the justification of the war is, after all, a matter for politicians and statesmen, and that the Church would be more appropriately employed in making it as far as she can a vehicle of good, rather than trying to justify, superfluously its existence. A people already awed by the self-sacrifice of its armies may be supposed to be capable of profiting by the exhortations of a Church whose cardinal doctrine is concerned with the responsibility that attaches to those for whose sake life has voluntarily been given up. One cannot imagine an institution more perfectly qualified by, its faith and its power to bring home to this people the solemnity of the sanction under which they lie to make themselves worthy of the price that is still being unreservedly paid. If it were consciously, the determination of every citizen to make himself worth dying for, who can doubt that a national unity of the sublimest kind would be within reach ?

Of all the influences which tend to rob the citizen of the sense of his birthright, perhaps one of the strongest, and yet the most subtle, is that of officialism. It seems inevitable that the enormously complex public services which are necessary in the modern State should set up a barrier between the private citizen and the official, whereby the true relation between them is obscured. The official loses his grasp of the fact that the mechanism of the State is established in the interests of the citizen ; the citizen comes to regard the State as a hostile institution, against which he has to defend himself. although it was made for his defence. It is a crime for him to cheat the State in the matter of tax-paying, it is no crime for the State to defraud him in excessive charges. Considered in the light of the fundamental relation of citizen and State, it seems incredible that in a democratic country it is possible for flourishing establishments to exist the sole business of which is to save the private individual from being defrauded by the tax-gathering bureaucracy. This is but a single and rather extreme example of the far-stretching segregation effected by the official machine. The slighter kinds of aloofness, of inhuman etiquette, of legalism and senseless dignity, of indifference to the individual, of devotion to formulæ and routine are no less powerful agents in depriving the common man of the sense of intimate reality in his citizenship which might be so valuable a source of national unity. If the official machine through its utmost parts were animated by an even moderately human spirit and used as a means of binding together the people, instead of as an engine of moral disruption, it might be of incalculable value in the strengthening of morale.

ENGLAND AGAINST GERMANY—GERMANY.

In an earlier part of this book the statement was made that the present juncture in human affairs probably forms one of those rare nodes of circumstance in which the making of an epoch in history, corresponds with a perceptible change in the secular progress of biological evolution.   It remains to attempt some justification of this opinion.

England and Germany face one another as perhaps the two most typical antagonists of the war.   It may, seem but a partial way of examining events if we limit our consideration to them.   Nevertheless, it is in this duel that the material we are concerned with is chiefly to be found, and it may be added Germany herself has abundantly distinguished this country as her typical foe—an instinctive judgment not without value.

By the end of September 1914 it had become reasonably clear that the war would be one of endurance, and the comparatively equal though fluctuating strength of the two groups of adversaries has since shown that in such endurance the main factor will be the moral factor rather than the material.   An examination of the moral strength of the two arch-enemies will therefore have the interest of life and death behind it, as well as such as may belong to the thesis which stands at the head of this chapter.

Germany affords a profoundly interesting study for the biological psychologist, and it is very important that we should not allow what clearness of representation we can get into our picture of her mind to be clouded by the heated atmosphere of national feeling in which our work must be done. As I have said elsewhere, it is merely to encourage fallacy to allow oneself to believe that one is without prejudices.   The most one can do is to recognize what prejudices are likely to exist and liberally, to allow for them.

If I were to say that at the present moment I can induce myself to believe that it will ever be possible for Europe to contain a strong Germany, of the current type and remain habitable by free peoples, the apparent absence of national bias in the statement would be a mere affectation, and by no means an evidence of freedom from prejudice. I am much more likely to get into reasonable relations with the truth if I admit to myself, quite frankly, my innermost conviction that the destruction of the German Empire is an indispensable preliminary to the making of a civilization tolerable by rational beings. Having recognized the existence of that belief as a necessary obstacle to complete freedom of thought, it may be possible to allow for it and to counteract what aberrations of judgment it may be likely to produce.

In making an attempt to estimate the relative moral resources of England and Germany at the present time it is necessary to consider them as biological entities or major units of the human species in the sense of that term we have already repeatedly used. We shall have to examine the evolutionary tendencies which each of these units has shown, and if possible to decide how far they have followed the lines of development which psychological theory indicates to be those of healthy, and progressive development for a gregarious animal.

I have already tried to show that the acquirement of the social habit by man—though in fact there is reason to believe that the social habit preceded and made possible his distinctively human characters —has committed him to an evolutionary process which is far from being completed yet, but which

nevertheless must be carried out to its consummation
if he is to escape increasingly, severe disadvantages
inherent in that biological type.   In other words, the
gregarious habit in an animal of large individual
mental capacity is capable of becoming, and indeed
must become a handicap rather than a bounty unless
the society, of the species undergoes a continuously,
progressive co-ordination which will enable it to
attract and absorb the energy, and activities of its
individual members.   We have seen that in a species
such as man, owing to the freedom from the direct
action of natural selection within the major unit, the
individual's capacity for varied reaction to his environment has undergone an enormous development,
while at the same time the capacity for intercommunication—upon which the co-ordination of the
major unit into a potent and frictionless mechanism
depends—has lagged far behind.   The term " intercommunication " is here used in the very widest
sense to indicate the ties that bind the individual
to his fellows and them to him.   It is not a very
satisfactory word.; but as might be expected in
attempting to express a series of functions so
complex and so unfamiliar to generalization, it is not
easy to find an exact expression ready made.
Another phrase applicable to a slightly different
aspect of the same function is " herd accessibility,"
which has the advantage of suggesting by its first
constituent the limitation, primitively at any rate, an
essential part of the capacities it is desired to denote.
The conception of herd accessibility includes the
specific sensitiveness of the individual to the
existence, presence, thought, and feelings of his
fellow-members of the major unit.; the power he
possesses of reacting in an altruistic and social mode
to stimuli which would necessarily evoke a merely
egoistic response from a non-social animal—that is
to say, the power to deflect and modify, egoistic

impulses into a social form without emotional loss or dissatisfaction ; the capacity to derive from the impulses of the herd a moral power in excess of any similar energy he may be able to develop from purely egoistic sources.

Intercommunication, the development of which of course depends upon herd-accessibility, enables the herd to act as a single creature whose power is greatly in excess of the sum of the powers of its individual members.

Intercommunication in the biological sense has, however, never been systematically cultivated by man, but has been allowed to develop haphazard and subject to all the hostile influences which must infest a society in which unregulated competition and selection are allowed to prevail. The extravagance of human life and labour, the indifference to suffering, the harshness and the infinite class segregation of human society are the result. The use of what I have called conscious direction is apparently the only means whereby this chaos can be converted into organized structure.

Outside the gregarious unit, the forms of organic life at any given time seem to be to some considerable extent determined by the fact that the pressure of environmental conditions and of competition tends to eliminate selectively the types which are comparatively unsuited to the conditions in which they find themselves. However much or little this process of natural selection has decided the course which the general evolutionary process has taken, there can be no doubt that it is a condition of animal life, and has an active influence. The suggestion may be hazarded that under circumstances natural selection tends rather to restrict variation instead of encouraging it as it has sometimes been supposed to do. When the external pressure is very severe it might be supposed that anything like free variation would be a serious disadvantage to a species, and if it persisted might result in actual extermination. It is conceivable, therefore, that natural selection is capable of favouring stable and non-progressive types at the expense of the variable and possibly " progressive," if such a term can be applied to species advancing towards extinction. Such a possible fixative action of natural selection is suggested by the fact that the appearance of mechanisms whereby the individual is protected from the direct action of natural selection seems to have led to an outburst of variation. In the multicellular animal the individual cells passing from under the direct pressure of natural selection become variable, and so capable of a very great specialization. In the gregarious unit the same thing happens, the individual member gaining freedom to vary and to become specialized without the risk that would have accompanied such an endowment in the solitary state.

Within the gregarious unit, then, natural selection in the strict sense is in abeyance, and the consequent freedom has allowed of a rich variety among the individual members. This variety provides the material from which an elaborate and satisfactory society might be constructed if there were any constant and discriminating influence acting upon it. Unfortunately, the forces at work in human society to-day are not of this kind, but are irregular in direction and fluctuating in strength, so that the material richness which would have been so valuable, had it been subject to a systematic and co-ordinate selection, has merely contributed to the confusion of the product. The actual mechanism by which society, while it has grown in strength and complexity, has also grown in confusion and disorder, is that peculiarity of the gregarious mind which automatically brings into the monopoly of power the mental type which I have called the stable and common opinion calls normal. This type supplies our most trusted politicians and officials, our bishops and headmasters, our successful lawyers and doctors, and all their trusty deputies, assistants, retainers, and faithful servants. Mental stability is their leading characteristic, they " know where they stand " as we say, they have a confidence in the reality of their aims and their position, an inaccessibility to new and strange phenomena, a belief in the established and customary, a capacity for ignoring what they regard as the unpleasant, the undesirable, and the improper, and a conviction that on the whole a sound moral order is perceptible in the universe and manifested in the progress of civilization. Such characteristics are not in the least inconsistent with the highest intellectual capacity, great energy and perseverance as well as kindliness, generosity, and patience, but they are in no way redeemed in social value by them.

In the year 1915 it is, unfortunately, in no way necessary to enumerate evidences of the confusion, the cruelty, the waste, and the weaknesses with which human society, under the guidance of minds of this type, has been brought to abound. Civilization through all its secular development under their rule has never acquired an organic unity of structure ; its defects have received no rational treatment, but have been concealed, ignored, and denied ; instead of being drastically rebuilt, it has been kept presentable by patches and buttresses, by paint, and putty, and whitewash. The building was already insecure, and now the storm has burst upon it, threatens incontinently to collapse.

The fact that European civilization, approaching what appeared to be the very meridian of its strength, could culminate in a disaster so frightful as the present war is proof that its development was radically unsound. This is by no means to say that the war could have been avoided by those immediately concerned. That is almost certainly not the case. The war was the consequence of inherent defects in the evolution of civilized life ; it was the consequence of human progress being left to chance, and to the interaction of the heterogeneous influences which necessarily arise within a gregarious unit whose individual members have a large power of varied reaction. In such an atmosphere minds essentially resistive alone can flourish and attain to power, and they are by their very qualities incapable of grasping the necessities of government or translating them into action.

The method of leaving the development of society to the confused welter of forces which prevail within it is now at last reduced to absurdity by the unmistakable teaching of events, and the conscious direction of man's destiny is plainly indicated by Nature as the only mechanism by which the social life of so complex an animal can be guaranteed against disaster and brought to yield its full possibilities.

A gregarious unit informed by conscious direction represents a biological mechanism of a wholly new type, a stage of advance in the evolutionary process capable of consolidating the supremacy of man and carrying to its full extent the development of his social instincts.

Such a directing intelligence or group of intelligences would take into account before all things the biological character of man, would understand that his condition is necessarily progressive along the lines of his natural endowments or downward to destruction. It would abandon the static view of society as something merely to be maintained, and adopt a more dynamic conception of statesmanship as something active, progressive, and experimental, reaching out towards new powers for human activity and new conquests for the human will.

It would discover what natural inclinations in man must be indulged, and would make them respectable, what inclinations in him must be controlled for the advantage of the species, and make them insignificant. It would cultivate intercommunication and altruism on the one hand, and bravery, boldness, pride, and enterprise on the other. It would develop national unity to a communion of interest and sympathy far closer than anything yet dreamed of as possible, and by doing so would endow the national unit with a self-control, fortitude, and moral power which would make it so obviously unconquerable that war would cease to be a possibility. To a people magnanimous, self-possessed, and open-eyed, unanimous in sentiment and aware of its strength, the conquest of fellow-nations would present its full futility. They would need for the acceptable exercise of their powers some more difficult, more daring, and newer task, something that stretches the human will and the human intellect to the limit of their capacity; the mere occupation and re-occupation of the stale and blood-drenched earth would be to them barbarians' work; time and space would be their quarry, destiny and the human soul the lands they would invade; they would sail their ships into the gulfs of the ether and lay tribute upon the sun and stars.

It is one of the features of the present crisis that gives to it its biological significance, that one of the antagonists—Germany—has discovered the necessity and value of conscious direction of the social unit. This is in itself an epoch-making event. Like many other human discoveries of similar importance, it has been incomplete, and it has not been accompanied by the corresponding knowledge of man and his natural history which alone could have given it full fertility and permanent value.

It seems to have been in no way a revelation of genius, and, indeed, the absence of any great profundity and scope of speculation is rather remarkable in the minds of the numerous German political philosophers. The idea would appear rather to have been developed out of the circumstances of the country, and to have been almost a habit before it became a conception. At any rate, its appearance was greatly favoured by the political conditions and history of the region in which it arose. If this had not been the case, 'it is scarcely conceivable that the principle could have been accepted so readily by the people, and in a form which was not without its asperities and its hardships for them, or that it could have been discovered without the necessary biological corollaries which are indispensable to the successful application of it.

Germany in some ways resembles a son who has been educated at home, and has taken up the responsibilities of the adult, and become bound by them without ever tasting the free intercourse of the school and university. She has never tasted the heady liquor of political liberty, she has had no revolution, and the blood of no political martyrs calls to her disturbingly from the ground. To such innocent and premature gravity the reasonable claims of what, after all, had to her the appearance of no more than an anxiously paternal Government could not fail to appeal.

Explain it how we may, there can be no doubt that to the German peoples the theoretical aspects of life have long had a very special appeal. Generalizations about national characteristics are notoriously fallacious, but it seems that with a certain reserve one may fairly say that there is a definite contrast in this particular between the Germans and, let us say, the English.

To minds of a theoretical bias the appeal of a

closely regulative type of Government, with all the advantages of organization which it possesses, must be very strong, and there is reason to believe that this fact has had influence in reconciling the people to the imposition upon it of the will of the Government.

Between a docile and intelligent people and a strong, autocratic, and intelligent Government the possibilities of conscious national direction could scarcely fail to become increasingly obvious and to be increasingly developed. A further and enormously potent factor in the progress of the idea was an immense accession of national feeling, derived from three almost bewilderingly successful wars, accomplished at surprisingly small cost, and culminating in a grandiose and no less successful scheme of unification. Before rulers and people an imperial destiny of unlimited scope, and allowing of unbounded dreams, now inevitably opened itself up. Alone, amongst the peoples of Europe, Germany saw herself a nation with a career. No longer disunited and denationalized, she had come into her inheritance. The circumstances of her rebirth were so splendid, the moral exaltation of her new unity was so great that she could scarcely but suppose that her state was the beginning of a career of further and unimagined glories and triumphs. There were not lacking enthusiastic and prophetic voices to tell her she was right.

The decade that followed the foundation of the Empire was, perhaps, more pregnant with destiny than that which preceded it, for it saw the final determination of the path which Germany was to follow. She had made the immense stride in the biological scale of submitting herself to conscious direction ; would she also follow the path which alone leads to a perfect concentration of national life and a permanent moral stability ?

To a nation with a purpose and a consciously realized destiny some principle of national unity is indispensable. Some strand of feeling which all can share, and in sharing which all can come into communion with one another, will be the framework on which is built up the structure of national energy and effort.

The reactions in which the social instinct manifests itself are not all equally developed in the different social species. It is true that there is a certain group of characteristics common to all social animals ; but it is also found that in one example there is a special development of one aspect of the instinct, while another example will show a characteristic development of a different aspect. Taking a broad survey of all gregarious types, we are able to distinguish three fairly distinct trends of evolution. We have the aggressive gregariousness of the wolf and dog, the protective gregariousness of the sheep and the ox, and, differing from both these, we have the more complex social structure of the bee and the ant, which we may call socialized gregariousness. The last-named is characterized by the complete absorption of the individual in the major unit, and the fact that the function of the social habit seems no longer to be the simple one of mere attack or defence, but rather the establishment of a State which shall be, as a matter of course, strong in defence and attack, but a great deal more than this as well. The hive is no mere herd or pack, but an elaborate mechanism for making use by co-ordinate and unified action of the utmost powers of the individual members. It is something which appears to be a complete substitute for individual existence, and as we have already said, seems like a new creature rather than a congeries united for some comparatively few and simple purposes. The hive and the ant's nest stand to the flock and the

pack as the fully organized multicellular animal
stands to the primitive zoogloea which is its fore-
runner. The wolf is united for attack, the sheep
is united for defence, but the bee is united for all
the activities and feelings of its life.

Socialized gregariousness is the goal of man's
development. A transcendental union with his
fellows is the destiny of the human individual,
and it is the attainment of this towards which the
constantly growing altruism of man is directed.
Poets and prophets have, at times, dimly seen this
inevitable trend of Nature, biology detects unmistakable evidence of it, and explains the slowness of
advance, which has been the despair of those others,
by the variety and power of man's mind, and
consoles us for the delay these qualities still cause
by the knowledge that they are guarantees of the
exactitude and completeness that the ultimate union
will attain.

When a nation takes to itself the idea of conscious
direction, as by a fortunate combination of circumstances Germany has been induced to do, it is
plain that some choice of a principle of national
unity will be its first and most important task. It
is plain, also, from the considerations we have just
laid down, that such a principle of national unity
must necessarily be a manifestation of the social
instinct, and that the choice is necessarily limited
to one of three types of social habit which
alone Nature has fitted gregarious animals to follow.
No nation has ever made a conscious choice amongst
these three types, but circumstances have led to
the adoption of one or another of them often enough
for history to furnish many suggestive instances.

The more or less purely aggressive or protective form has been adopted for the most part by
primitive peoples. The history of the natives of
North America and Australia furnishes examples of

almost pure types of both. The aggressive type was illustrated very fully by the peoples who profited by the disintegration of the Roman Empire. These northern barbarians showed in the most perfect form the lupine type of society in action. The ideals and feelings exemplified by their sagas are comprehensible only when one understands the biological significance of them. It was a society of wolves marvellously indomitable in aggression but fitted for no other activity in any corresponding degree, and always liable to absorption by the peoples they had conquered. They were physically brave beyond belief, and made a religion of violence and brutality. To fight was for them man's supreme activity. They were restless travellers and explorers, less out of curiosity than in search of prey, and they irresistibly overran Europe in the missionary zeal of the sword and torch, each man asking nothing of Fate but, after a career of unlimited outrage and destruction, to die gloriously fighting. It is impossible not to recognize the psychological identity of these ideals with those which we might suppose a highly developed breed of wolves to entertain.

With all its startling energy, and all its magnificent enterprise, the lupine type of society has not proved capable of prolonged survival. Probably its inherent weakness is the very limited scope of interest it provides for active and progressive minds, and the fact that it tends to engender a steadily accumulating hostility in weaker but more mentally progressive peoples to which it has no correspondingly steady resistiveness to oppose.

The history of the world has shown a gradual elimination of the lupine type. It has recurred sporadically at intervals, but has always been suppressed. Modern civilization has shown a constantly increasing manifestation of the socialized type of gregariousness in spite of the complexities and disorders which the slowness of its development towards completeness has involved. It may be regarded now as the standard type which has been established by countless experiments, as that which alone can satisfy and absorb the moral as well as the intellectual desires of modern man.

From the point of view of the statesman desiring to enforce an immediate and energetic national unity, combined with an ideal of the State as destined to expand into a larger and larger sphere, the socialized type of gregarious evolution is extremely unsatisfactory. Its course towards the production of a truly organized State is slow, and perplexed by a multitudinous confusion of voices and ideals ; its necessary development of altruism gives the society it produces an aspect of sentimentality and flabbiness ; its tendency slowly to evolve towards the moral equality of its members gives the State an appearance of structural insecurity.

If Germany was to be capable of a consistent aggressive external policy as a primary aim, the peculiarity of her circumstances rendered her unable to seek national inspiration by any development of the socialized type of instinctive response, because that method can produce the necessary moral power only through a true unity of its members, such as implies a moral, if not a material, equality among them. That the type is capable of yielding a passion of aggressive nationalism is shown by the early enterprise and conquests of the first French Republic. But that outburst of power was attained only because it was based on a true, though doubtless imperfect, moral equality. Such a method was necessarily forbidden to the German Empire by the intense rigidity of its social segregation, with its absolute differentiation between the aristocracy and the common people. In such a society there could be no thought of permitting the faintest hint of even moral equality.

This is the reason, therefore, why the rulers of Germany, of course in complete ignorance of how significant was their choice, were compelled to abandon the ideals of standard civilization, to relapse upon the ideals of a more primitive type of gregariousness, and to throw back their people into the anachronism of a lupine society. In this connection it is interesting to notice how persistently the political philosophers of Germany have sought their chief inspiration in the remote past, and in times when the wolf society and the wolf ideals were widespread and successful.

It is not intended to imply that there was here any conscious choice. It is remarkable enough that the rulers of Germany recognized the need for conscious direction of all the activities of a nation which proposes for itself a career ; it would have been a miracle if they had understood the biological significance of the differentiation of themselves from other European peoples that they, were to bring about. To them it doubtless appeared merely that they, were discarding the effete and enfeebling ideals which made other nations the fit victims of their conquests. They may be supposed to have determined to eradicate such germs of degeneracy, from themselves, to have seen that an ambitious people must be strong and proud and hard, enterprising, relentless, brave, and fierce, prepared to believe in the glory of combat and conquest, in the supreme moral greatness of the warrior, in force as the touchstone of right, honour, justice, and truth. Such changes in moral orientation seem harmless enough, and it can scarcely be suspected that their significance was patent to those who adopted them. They were impressed upon the nation with all the immense power of suggestion at the disposal of an organized State. The readiness with which they were received and assimilated was more than could be accounted for by even the power of the immense machine of officials, historians, theologians, professors, teachers, and newspapers by which they were, in season and out of season, enforced. The immense success that was attained owed much to the fact that suggestion was following a natural, instinctive path. The wolf in man, against which civilization has been fighting for so long, is still within call and ready to respond to incantations much feebler than those the German State could employ. The people were intoxicated with the glory of their conquests and their imposing new confederation ; if we are to trust the reputation the Prussian soldier has had for a hundred years, they were perhaps already less advanced in humanity than the other European peoples. The fact is unquestionable that they followed their teachers with enthusiasm.

It may be well for us, before proceeding farther, to define precisely the psychological hypothesis we are advancing in explanation of the peculiarities of the German national character as now manifested.

Herd instinct is manifested in three distinct types, the aggressive, the protective, and the socialized, which are exemplified in Nature by the wolf, the sheep, and the bee respectively. Either type can confer the advantages of the social habit, but the socialized is that upon which modern civilized man has developed. It is maintained here that the ambitious career consciously planned for Germany by those who had taken command of her destinies, and the maintenance at the same time of her social system, were inconsistent with the further development of gregariousness of the socialized type. New ideals, new motives, and new sources of moral power had therefore to be sought. They were found in a recrudescence of the aggressive type of gregariousness—in a reappearance of the society of the wolf. It is conceivable that those who provided Germany with her new ideals thought themselves to be exercising a free choice. The choice, however, was forced upon them by Nature. They wanted some of the characters of the wolf ; they got them all. One may imagine that those who have so industriously inculcated the national gospel have wondered at times that while it has been easy to implant certain of the desired ideals, it has not been possible to prevent the appearance of others which, though not so desirable, belong to the same legacy, and must be taken up with it.

Before examining the actual mental features of Germany to-day, it may be desirable to consider *a priori* what would be the mental characteristics of an aggressive gregarious animal were he to be self-conscious in the sense that man is.

The functional value of herd instinct in the wolf is to make the pack irresistible in attacking and perpetually aggressive in spirit. The individual must, therefore, be especially sensitive to the leadership of the herd. The herd must be to him, not merely as it is to the protectively gregarious animal, a source of comfort, and stimulus, and general guidance, but must be able to make him *do things* however difficult, however dangerous, even however senseless, and must make him yield an absolute, immediate, and slavish obedience. The carrying out of the commands of the herd must be in itself an absolute satisfaction in which there can be no consideration of self. Towards anything outside the herd he will necessarily be arrogant, confident, and inaccessible to the appeals of reason or feeling. This tense bond of instinct, constantly keyed up to the pitch of action, will give him a certain simplicity of character and even ingenuousness, a coarseness and brutality in his dealings with others, and a complete failure to understand any motive unsanctioned by the pack. He will believe the pack to be impregnable and irresistible, just and good, and will readily ascribe to it any other attribute which may take his fancy however ludicrously inappropriate.

The strength of the wolf pack as a gregarious unit is undoubtedly, in suitable circumstances, enormous. This strength would seem to depend on a continuous possibility of attack and action. How far it can be maintained in inactivity, and mere defence is another matter. . . .

Since the beginning of this war attracted a really concentrated attention to the psychology of the German people, it has been very obvious that one of the most striking feelings amongst Englishmen has been bewilderment. They have found an indescribable strangeness in the utterances of almost all German personages and newspapers, in their diplomacy, in their friendliness to such as they wished to propitiate, in their enmity to those they wished to alarm and intimidate. This strange quality is very difficult to define or even to attempt to describe, and has very evidently perplexed almost all writers on the war. The only thing one can be sure of is that it is there. It shows itself at times as a simplicity or even childishness, as a boorish cunning, as an incredible ant-like activity, as a sudden blast of maniacal boasting, a reckless savagery, of gloating in blood, a simple-minded sentimentality, as outbursts of idolatry, not of the pallid, metaphorical, modern type, but the full-blooded African kind, with all the apparatus of idol and fetish and tom-tom, and with it all a steady confidence that these are the principles of civilization, of truth, of justice, and of Christ.

I have tried to put down at random some of the factors in this curious impression as they occur to the memory, but the mere enumeration of them is not possible without risking the objective composure of one's attitude—an excellent incidental evidence that the strangeness is a reality.

The incomprehensibility to the English of the whole trend of German feeling and expression suggests that there is some deeply rooted instinctive conflict of attitude between them. One may risk the speculation that this conflict is between socialized gregariousness and aggressive gregariousness. As the result of the inculcation of national arrogance and aggression, Germany has lapsed into a special type of social instinct which has opened a gulf of separation in feeling between her and other civilized peoples. Such an effect is natural enough. Nothing produces the sense of strangeness so much as differences of instinctive reaction. A similar though wider gap in instinctive reaction gives to us the appearance of strangeness and queerness in the behaviour of the cat as contrasted with the dog, which is so much more nearly allied in feeling to ourselves.

If, then, we desire to get any insight into the mind and moral power of Germany, we must begin with the realization that the two peoples are separated by a profound difference in instinctive feeling. Nature has provided but few roads for gregarious species to follow. Between the path England finds herself in and that which Germany has chosen there is a divergence which almost amounts to a specific difference in the biological scale. In this, perhaps, lies the cause of the desperate and unparalleled ferocity of this war. It is a war not so much of contending nations as of contending species. We are not taking part in a mere war, but in one of Nature's august experiments. It is as if she had

set herself to try out in her workshop the strength
of the socialized and the aggressive types. To
the socialized peoples she has entrusted the task
of proving that her old faith in cruelty and blood
is at last an anachronism. To try them, she has
given substance to the creation of a nightmare, and
they must destroy this werewolf or die.[1]

In attempting to estimate the actual phenomena
of the German mind at the present time, we must
remember that our sources of knowledge are subject
to a rigid selection. Those of us who are unable to
give time to the regular reading of German publications must depend on extracts which owe their
appearance in our papers to some striking characteristic which may be supposed to be pleasing
to the prejudices or hopes of the English reader.
The main facts, however, are clear enough to yield

[1] It may be noted that the members of the small group of so-called
"pro-German" writers and propagandists for the most part make
it a fundamental doctrine, either explicit or implicit, that there is no
psychological difference between the English and the Germans.
They seem to maintain that the latter are moved and are to be
influenced by exactly the same series of feelings and ideals as the
former, and show in reality no observable "strangeness" in their
expressions and emotions. By arguments based on this assumption
very striking conclusions are reached. All moral advancement has
been the work of unpopular minorities, the members of which have
been branded as cranks or criminals until time has justified their
doctrine. Even the greatest of such pioneers have not, however, been
invariably right. Their genius has usually been shown most clearly in
matters with which they have been most familiar, while in matters
less intimately part of their experience their judgments have often not
stood the test of time any better than those of smaller men. If therefore our "pro-Germans" include amongst them men of moral genius,
we may expect that such of their psychological intuitions as deal with
England are more likely to prove true than those that deal with
Germany. The importance of this reservation lies in the probability
that the chief psychological problems connected with the origin and
prosecution of this war relate to the Germans rather than to the
English.

valuable conclusions, if such are made on broad lines without undue insistence on minor points.

An intense but often ingenuous and even childish national arrogance is a character that strikes one at once. It seems to be a serious and often a solemn emotion impregnably armoured against the comic sense, and expressed with a childlike confidence in its justness. It is usually associated with a language of metaphor, which is almost always florid and banal, and usually grandiose and strident. This fondness for metaphor and inability to refer to common things by plain names affects all classes, from Emperor to journalist, and gives an impression of peculiar childishness. It reminds one of the primitive belief in the transcendental reality, and value of names.

The national arrogance of the German is at the same time peculiarly sensitive and peculiarly obtuse. It is readily moved by praise or blame, though that be the most perfunctory and this the most mild, but it has no sense of a public opinion outside the pack. It is easily aroused to rage by external criticism, and when it finds its paroxysms make it ridiculous to the spectator it cannot profit by the information but becomes, if possible, more angry. It is quite unable to understand that to be moved to rage by an enemy is as much a proof of slavish automatism as to be moved to fear by him. The really extraordinary hatred for England is, quite apart from the obvious association of its emotional basis with fear, a most interesting phenomenon. The fact that it was possible to organize so unanimous a howl shows very clearly how fully the psychological mechanisms of the wolf were in action. It is most instructive to find eminent men of science and philosophers bristling and baring their teeth with the rest, and would be another proof, if such were needed, of the infinite insecurity of the hold of reason in the most carefully cultivated minds when it is opposed by strong herd feeling.[1]

It is important, however, not to judge the functional value of these phenomena of herd arrogance and herd irritability and convulsive rage from the point of view of nations of the socialized gregarious type such as ourselves. To us they would be disturbants of judgment, and have no corresponding emotional recompense. In the wolf pack, however, they are indigenous, and represent a normal mechanism for inciting national enthusiasm and unity. The wolf, whose existence depends on the daily exercise of pursuit and slaughter, cannot afford

[1] I have not included in these pages actual quotations from German authors illustrative of the national characteristics they so richly display. Such material may be found in abundance in the many books upon Germany which have appeared since the beginning of the war. The inclusion of it here would therefore have been superfluous, and would have tended perhaps to distract attention from the more general aspects of the subject which are the main objects of this study. During the process of final revision I am, however, tempted to add a single illustration which happens just to have caught my eye as being a representative and not at all an extreme example of the national arrogance I refer to above.

In an article on "The German Mind" by Mr. John Buchan I find the following quotations from a Professor Werner Sombart, of Berlin :—

"When the German stands leaning on his mighty sword, clad in steel from his sole to his head, whatsoever will may, down below, dance around his feet, and the intellectuals and the learned men of England, France, Russia, and Italy may rail at him and throw mud. But in his lofty repose he will not allow himself to be disturbed, and he will reflect in the sense of his old ancestors in Europe : *Oderint dum metuant.*"

"We must purge from our soul the last fragments of the old ideal of a progressive development of humanity. . . . The ideal of humanity can only be understood in its highest sense when it attains its highest and richest development in particular noble nations. These for the time being are the representatives of God's thought on earth. Such were the Jews. Such were the Greeks. And the chosen people of these centuries is the German people. . . . Now we understand why other peoples pursue us with their hatred. They do

to be open to external appeals and criticisms, must be supremely convinced of his superiority and that whoever dies he must live, and must be easily stimulated to the murderous rages by which he wins his food.

Another difficulty in the understanding of the German mind is its behaviour with regard to influencing non-German opinion. There can be no doubt that it desires intensely to create impressions

not understand us, but they are sensible of our enormous spiritual superiority. So the Jews were hated in antiquity because they were the representatives of God on earth " (" The German Mind," *Land and Water*, November 6, 1915).

These passages are almost too good to be true, and give one some of the pleasure of the collector who finds a perfect specimen. Here we have the gusto in childish and banal metaphor, the conception of the brutal conqueror's state as permanently blissful—the colonizing principle of Prussia—the naïve generalizations from history, the confident assumption of any characteristic which appears desirable in morals or religion, the impenetrable self-esteem, and I think we should add the intense and honest conviction.

If we judge from the standpoint of our own feelings and ideals such utterances as these, we cannot ignore the maniacal note in them, and we seem forced to assume some actually lunatic condition in the German people. Indeed, this is a conclusion which Mr. Buchan in the article from which I quote does not hesitate definitely and persuasively to draw.

When we remember, however, that the definition of insanity is necessarily a statistical one, that in the last analysis we can but say that a madman is a man who behaves differently from the great bulk of his neighbours, we find that to describe a nation as mad—true as it may be in a certain sense—leaves us without much addition to our knowledge. In so far, however, as it impresses upon us the fact that some of that nation's mental processes are fundamentally different from our own it is a useful conception. The statesman will do well to carry the analysis a stage farther. The ravings of a maniac do not help us much in forecasting his behaviour, the howlings of a pack of wolves, equally irrational, equally harsh, even, in the original sense, equally lunatic, betray to us with whom we have to deal, betray their indispensable needs, their uncontrollable passions, the narrow path of instinct n which they are held, enable us to foresee, and, foreseeing, to lay our plans.

favourable to itself, not merely for the sake of
practical advantages in conducting the war, but also
because of the desire for sympathy. In considering the latter motive it is important that one's
attention should not be too much attracted by the
comic aspects of the searchings of heart, publicly
indulged by Germans, as to why they are not
regarded with a more general and sincere affection,
and of the answers which they themselves have
furnished to this portentous problem. That they
are too modest, too true, too self-obliterating, too
noble, too brave, and too kind are answers the
psychological significance of which should not be
altogether lost in laughter. That they are honest
expressions of belief cannot be doubted ; indeed,
there is strong theoretical reason to accept them
as such, when we remember the fabulous[1] impenetrability of lupine herd suggestion. In default of
such an explanation they seem to be utterly incomprehensible.

In her negotiations with other peoples, and her
estimates of national character, Germany shows the
characteristic features of her psychological type in
a remarkable way. It appears to be a principal
thesis of hers that altruism is, for the purposes of
the statesman, non-existent, or if it exists is an
evidence of degeneracy and a source of weakness.
The motives upon which a nation acts are, according
to her, self-interest and fear, and in no particular
has her " strangeness " been more fully shown than
in the frank way in which she appeals to both,
either alternately or together.

This disbelief in altruism, and over-valuation of
fear and self-interest, seem to be regarded by her

---

[1] The use of this adjective may perhaps call to mind how often the
wolf has appeared in fable in just this mood. Usually, however, the
fabulist—being of the unsympathetic socialized type—has ascribed the
poor creature's yearnings to hypocrisy.

as evidence of a fearless and thorough grasp of biological truth, and are often fondly referred to as " true German objectivity " or the German " sense for reality." How grossly, in fact, they conflict with the biological theory of gregariousness is clear enough. It is interesting that the German negotiators have been almost uniformly unsuccessful in imposing their wishes on States in which the socialized type of gregariousness is highly developed —Italy, the United States—and have succeeded with barbarous peoples of the lupine type, with the Turk, whose " objectivity " and appetite for massacre remain ever fresh, patriarch among wolves as he is, with Bulgaria, the wolf of the second Balkan War.

There is strong reason to believe that defective insight into the minds of others is one of the chief disadvantages of the aggressive as compared with the socialized type of gregariousness. This disadvantage is so great, and yet so deeply inherent, as to justify the belief that the type is the most primitive of those now surviving, and that its present resuscitation in man is a phenomenon which will prove to be no more than transient.

It would be of little value to enumerate the well-known instances in which failure of insight, and ignorance of the psychology of the herd, has been misleading or disadvantageous to Germany. It is relevant, however, to note the superb illustration of psychological principle which is afforded by the relations of Germany to England during the last fifteen years. That England was the great obstacle to indefinite expansion was clearly understood by those whom the conception of a consciously directed and overwhelmingly powerful German Empire had inspired. I have tried to show how great a conception this was, how truly in the line of natural evolution, how it marks an epoch even on the biological scale. Unfortunately for Germany, her social

type was already fixed, with such advantages and
defects as it possessed, and amongst them the
immense defect of the lupine attitude towards an
enemy—the over-mastering temptation to intimidate
him rather than to understand, and to accept the easy
and dangerous suggestions of hostility in estimating
his strength.

There is in the whole of human history, perhaps
no more impressive example of the omnipotence
of instinct than that which is afforded by the
reactions of Germany towards England. An intelligent, educated, organized people, directed consciously towards a definite ambition, finds its path
blocked by an enemy in chief. Surely there are
two principles of action which should at once be
adopted : first, to estimate with complete objectivity
the true strength of the enemy, and to allow no
national prejudice, no liking for pleasant prophesy-
ing to distort the truth, and secondly, to guard
against exasperating the enemy, lest the inevitable
conflict should ultimately be precipitated by her
at her moment.

Both these principles the instinctive impulsions
to which Germany was liable compelled her to
violate. She allowed herself to accept opinions
of England's strength, moral and physical, which
were pleasant rather than true. She listened eagerly
to political philosophers and historians—the most
celebrated of whom was, by an ominous coincidence,
deaf—who told her that the Empire of England
was founded in fraud and perpetuated in feebleness,
that it consisted of a mere loose congeries of disloyal
peoples who would fly asunder at the first touch of
" reality," that it was rotten with insurgency, senile
decay and satiety, and would not and could not
fight. Even if these things had been a full statement of the case, they must have been dangerous
doctrines. They were defective because the

observers were unaware that they were studying different instinctive reactions from their own, and were, therefore, deaf to the notes which might have put them on their guard.

At the same time, Germany allowed herself to indulge the equally pleasant expression of her hostility with a freedom apparently unrestrained by any knowledge that such indulgences cannot be enjoyed for nothing. She produced in this country a great deal of alarm, and a great deal of irritation, an effect she no doubt regarded as gratifying, but which made it quite certain that sooner or later England would recognize her implacable enemy, though, inarticulate as usual, she might not say much about it. . . .

Another feature of Germany's social type, which has an important bearing on her moral strength, is the relation of the individual citizens to one another. The individual of the wolf pack is of necessity fierce, aggressive, and irritable, otherwise he cannot adequately fulfil his part in the major unit. Apparently it is beyond the power of Nature to confine the ferocity of the wolf solely to the external activities of the pack, as would obviously be in many ways advantageous, and to a certain extent therefore it affects the relations of members of the pack to one another. This is seen very well even in the habits of domesticated dogs, who are apt to show more or less suppressed suspicion and irritability towards one another even when well acquainted, an irritability moreover which is apt to blaze out into hostility on very slight provocation.

Most external commentators on modern German life have called attention to the harshness which is apt to pervade social relations. They tell us of an atmosphere of fierce competition, of ruthless scandal-

mongering and espionage, of insistence upon minute
distinctions of rank and title, of a rigid ceremonious
politeness which obviously has little relation to
courtesy, of a deliberate cultivation by superiors
of a domineering harshness towards their inferiors,
of habitual cruelty to animals, and indeed of the
conscious, deliberate encouragement of harshness
and hardness of manner and feeling as laudable
evidences of virility. The statistics of crime, the
manners of officials, the tone of newspapers, the
ferocious discipline of the Army, and the general
belief that personal honour is stained by endurance
and purified by brutality are similar phenomena.

Nothing in this category, however, is more
illuminating than the treatment by Germany of
colonies and conquered territories. To the English
the normal method of treating a conquered country,
is to obliterate, as soon as possible, every trace
of conquest, and to assimilate the inhabitants to
the other citizens of the empire by every possible
indulgence of liberty and self-government. It is,
therefore, difficult for him to believe that the German
actually likes to be reminded that a given province
has been conquered, and is not unwilling that a
certain amount of discontent and restiveness in the
inhabitants should give him opportunities of forcibly,
exercising his dominion and resuscitating the glories
of conquest. Although this fact has no doubt been
demonstrated countless times, it was first displayed
unmistakably to the world in the famous Zabern
incident. Those who have studied the store of
psychological material furnished by that affair, the
trial and judgments which followed it, and the
ultimate verdict of the people thereon, cannot fail
to have reached the conclusion that here is exposed
in a crucial experiment a people which is either
totally incomprehensible, or is responding to the
calls of herd instinct by a series of reactions almost

totally different from those we regard as normal.
When the biological key to the situation is discovered the series of events otherwise bizarre to
the pitch of incredibility becomes not only intelligible and consistent, but also inevitable.

The differences in instinctive social type between
Germany and England are betrayed in many minor
peculiarities of behaviour that cannot be examined
or even enumerated here.   Some of them are of
little importance in themselves, though all of them
are significant when the whole bulk of evidence
to which they contribute a share is considered.
Indeed, some of the less obviously important characteristics, by the very nicety with which they fulfil
the conditions demanded by the biological necessities
of the case, have a very special value as evidence
in favour of the generalizations which I have
suggested.   I permit myself an illustration of this
point.   The use of war cries and shibboleths doubtless seems in itself an insignificant subject enough,
yet I think an examination of it can be shown to
lead directly to the very central facts of the
international situation.

Few phenomena have been more striking throughout the war than the way in which the German
people have been able to take up certain cries—
directed mostly against England—and bring them
into hourly familiar and unanimous use.   The phrase
" God punish England ! " seems actually to have
attained a real and genuine currency, and to have
been used by all classes and all ages as a greeting
with a solemnity and gusto which are in no way the
less genuine for being, to our unsympathetic eyes, so
ludicrous.   The famous " Hymn of Hate " had, no
doubt, a popularity equally wide, and was used with
a fervour which showed the same evidence of a
mystic satisfaction.

Attempts have been made to impose upon England

similar watchwords with the object of keeping some
of the direst events of the war before our eyes, and
fortifying the intensity and scope of our horror.
We have been adjured to "remember" Belgium,
Louvain, the *Lusitania*, and latterly the name of
an heroic and savagely murdered nurse. Horrible
as has been the crime to which we have been
recalled by each of these phrases, there has never
been the slightest sign that the memory of it could
acquire a general currency of quotation, and by that
mechanism become a stronger factor in unity
determination or endurance.

An allied phenomenon which may perhaps be mentioned here is the difference in attitude of the
German and the English soldier towards war songs.
To the German the war song is a serious matter ; it
is for the most part a grave composition, exalted
in feeling, and thrilling with the love of country ;
he is taught to sing it, and he sings it well, with
obvious and touching sincerity and with equally,
obvious advantage to his morale.

The attempt to introduce similar songs and a
similar attitude towards them to the use of the
English soldier has often been made, and exactly
as often lamentably failed. On the whole it has
been, perhaps, the most purely comic effort of the
impulse to mimic Germany which has been in favour
until of late with certain people of excellent aims
but inadequate biological knowledge. The English
soldier, consistently preferring the voice of Nature
to that of the most eminent doctrinaire, has, to the
scandal of his lyrical enemies, steadily drawn his
inspiration from the music-hall and the gutter, or
from his own rich store of flippant and ironic
realism.

The biological meaning of these peculiarities
renders them intelligible and consistent with one
another. The predaceous social animals in attack

or pursuit are particularly sensitive to the encouragement afforded by one another's voices. The pack
gives tongue because of the functional value of the
exercise, which is clearly of importance in keeping
individuals in contact with one another, and in
stimulating in each the due degree of aggressive
rage. That serious and narrow passion tends
naturally to concentrate itself upon some external
object or quarry, which becomes by the very fact an
object of hate to the exclusion of any other feeling,
whether of sympathy, self-possession, or a sense of
the ludicrous. The curious spectacle of Germans
greeting one another with " God punish England ! "
and the appropriate response is therefore no accidental or meaningless phenomenon, but a manifestation of an instinctive necessity ; and this explanation
is confirmed by the immensely wide currency of the
performance, and the almost simian gravity with
which it could be carried out. It succeeded because
it had a functional value, just as similar movements
in England have failed because they have had no
functional value, and could have none in a people of
the socialized type, with whom unity depends on a
different kind of bond.

The wolf, then, is the father of the war song,
and it is among peoples of the lupine type alone that
the war song is used with real seriousness. Animals
of the socialized type are not dependent for their
morale upon the narrow intensities of aggressive
rage. Towards such manifestations of it as concerted cries and war songs they feel no strong
instinctive impulsion, and are therefore able to
preserve a relatively objective attitude. Such
cryings of the pack, seeming thus to be mere
functionless automatisms, naturally enough come to
be regarded as patently absurd.

Examples of behaviour illustrating these deep
differences of reaction are often to be met with in the

stories of those who have described incidents of the war. It is recorded that German soldiers in trenches within hearing of the English, seeking to exasperate and appal the latter, have sung in an English version their fondly valued " Hymn of Hate." Whereupon the English, eagerly listening and learning the words of the dreadful challenge, have petrified their enemies by repeating it with equal energy and gusto, dwelling no doubt with the appreciation of experts upon the curses of their native land.

It would scarcely be possible to imagine a more significant demonstration of the psychological differences of the two social types.

The peculiarities of a state of the wolfish type are admirably suited to conditions of aggression and conquest, and readily yield for those purposes a maximal output of moral strength. As long as such a nation is active and victorious in war, its moral resources cannot fail, and it will be capable of an indefinite amount of self-sacrifice, courage, and energy. Take away from it, however, the opportunities of continued aggression, interrupt the succession of victories by a few heavy defeats, and it must inevitably lose the perfection of its working as an engine of moral power. The ultimate and singular source of *inexhaustible* moral power in a gregarious unit is the perfection of communion amongst its individual members. As we have seen, this source is undeveloped in units of the aggressive type, and has been deliberately ignored by Germany. As soon, if ever, as she has to submit to a few unmistakable defeats in the field, as soon as, if it should happen, all outlets for fresh aggression are closed, she will become aware of how far she has staked her moral resources on continuous success, and will not be able for long to conceal her knowledge from the world.

That she herself has always been dimly aware of the nature of her strength—though not perhaps of her potential weakness—is shown by her steady insistence upon the necessity of aggression, upon maintaining the attack at whatever cost of life. This is a principle she has steadily acted upon throughout the war. It is exemplified by the whole series of terrible lunges at her enemies she has made. The strategic significance of these has, perhaps, become less as the moral necessity for them has become greater. France, Flanders, Russia, and the Balkans have in turn had to supply the moral food of victory and attack without which she would soon have starved. There is a quality at which the imagination cannot but be appalled in this fate of a great and wonderful nation, however much her alienation of herself from the instincts of mankind may have frozen the natural currents of pity. Panting with the exhaustion of her frightful blow at Russia, she must yet turn with who knows what weariness to yet another enterprise, in which to find the moral necessities which the Russian campaign was already ceasing to supply. It is to a similar mechanism that we must look to trace the ultimate source of the submarine and aircraft campaigns against England. Strategically, these proceedings may or may not have been regarded hopefully ; possibly they were based on a definite military plan, though they do not to us have that appearance. Very probably they were expected to disorganize English morale. Behind them both, however, whether consciously or not, was the moral necessity to do something against England. This is indicated by the circumstances and the periods of the war at which they were seriously taken up. As both the submarine and the Zeppelin campaigns involve no great expenditure or dissipation of power, the fact that their value is moral rather than military, and concerned with the morale of their inventors rather than that of their victims, is chiefly of academic interest as throwing further light on the nature of Germany's strength and weakness.

Its attitude towards discipline displays the German mind in a relation sufficiently instructive to merit some comment here. When Germany has been reproached with being contented to remain in what is, by comparison with other peoples, a condition of political infantilism, with allowing the personal liberty of her citizens to be restricted on all hands, and their political responsibility to be kept within the narrowest limits, the answer of the political theorists has generally contained two distinct and contradictory apologetic theses. It has been said that the German, recognizing the value of State organization, and that strict discipline is a necessary preliminary to it, consciously resigns the illusory privileges of the democrat in order to gain power, and submits to a kind of social contract which is unquestionably advantageous in the long run. The mere statement of such a proposition is enough to refute it, and we need give no further attention to an intellectualist fallacy so venerable and so completely inconsistent with experience. It is also said, however, that the German has a natural aptitude for discipline amounting to genius. In a sense a little less flattering than it is intended to have, this proposition is as true as that of the social contract is false. The aggressive social type lends itself naturally to discipline, and shows it in its grossest forms. The socialized type is, of course, capable of discipline, otherwise a State would be impossible, but the discipline that prevails in it is apt to become indirect, less harshly compulsory and more dependent on goodwill.

It is perhaps natural that units within which

ferocity and hardness are tolerated and encouraged
should depend on a correspondingly savage method
of enforcing their will. The flock of sheep has its
shepherd, but the pack of hounds has its *Whips*.
In human societies of the same type we should
expect to find, therefore, a general acquiescence in
the value of discipline, and a toleration of its enforcement, because, rather than in spite of, its being
harsh. This seems to be the mechanism which
underlies what is to the Englishman the mystery
of German submission to direction and discipline.
That an able-bodied soldier should submit to being
lashed across the face by his officer for some trivial
breach of etiquette—a type of incident common and
well witnessed to—is evidence of a state of mind
in *both* parties utterly incomprehensible to our feelings. The hypothesis I am suggesting would explain
it by comparison with the only available similar
phenomenon—the submission of a dog to a thrashing administered by his master. The dog illustrates very well that in a predaceous social animal
the enforcement of a harsh and even brutal discipline
is not only a possible but also a perfectly satisfactory procedure in the psychological sense. That
other common victim of man's brutality—the horse
—provides an interesting complement to the proposition by showing that in a protectively social animal
a savage enforcement of discipline is psychologically
unsatisfactory. It seems justifiable, therefore, to
conclude that the aggressive gregariousness of the
Germans is the instinctive source of the marvellous
discipline of their soldiers, and the contribution it
makes to their amazing bravery. It must not be
taken as any disrespect for that wonderful quality,
but as a desire to penetrate as far as possible into
its meaning, that compels one to point out that
the theoretical considerations I have advanced are
confirmed by the generally admitted dependence of

the German soldier on his officers and the at least respectably attested liability he shows to the indulgence of an inhuman savagery towards any one who is not his master by suggestion or by force of arms.

In the attempt I have made to get some insight into the German mind, and to define the meaning of its ideals, and needs, and impulses in biological terms, I have had to contend with the constant bias one has naturally been influenced by in discussing a people not only intensely hostile, but also animated by what I have tried to show is an alien type of the social habit. Nevertheless, there seem to be certain broad conclusions which may be usefully recalled in summary here as constituting reasonable probabilities. My purpose will have been effected if these are sufficiently consistent to afford a point of view slightly different from the customary one, and yielding some practical insight into the facts.

Germany presents to the biological psychologist the remarkable paradox of being in the first place a State consciously directed towards a definite series of ideals and ambitions, and deliberately organized to obtain them, and in the second place a State in which prevails a primitive type of the gregarious instinct—the aggressive—a type which shows the closest resemblance in its needs, its ideals, and its reactions to the society of the wolf pack. Thus she displays, in one respect, what I have shown to be the summit of gregarious evolution, and in another its very antithesis—a type of society which has always been transient, and has failed to satisfy the needs of modern civilized man.

When I compare German society with the wolf pack, and the feelings, desires, and impulses of the individual German with those of the wolf or dog, I am not intending to use a vague analogy, but

to call attention to a real and gross identity. The
aggressive social animal has a complete and consistent series of psychical reactions, which will necessarily be traceable in his feelings and his behaviour,
whether he is a biped or a quadruped, a man or
an insect. The psychical necessity that makes the
wolf brave in a massed attack is the same as that
which makes the German brave in a massed attack ;
the psychical necessity which makes the dog submit
to the whip of his master and profit by it makes
the German soldier submit to the lash of his officer
and profit by it. The instinctive process which
makes the dog among his fellows irritable, sus-
picious, ceremonious, sensitive about his honour, and
immediately ready to fight for it is identical in
the German and produces identical effects.

The number and minuteness of the coincidences
of behaviour between the German and other aggressive social species, the number and precision of
the differences between the German and the other
types of social animals make up together a body
of evidence which is difficult to ignore.

Moreover, we see Germany compelled to submit
to disadvantages, consequent upon her social type,
which, we may suppose, she would have avoided
had they not been too deeply ingrained for even
her thoroughness to remove. Thus she is unable
to make or keep friends amongst nations of the
socialized type ; her instinctive valuation of fear
as a compelling influence has allowed her to indulge
the threatenings and warlike gestures which have
alienated all the strong nations, and intimidated
successfully only the weak—England, for example,
is an enemy entirely of her own making ; she
has been forced to conduct the war on a plan
of ceaseless and frightfully costly aggression,
because her morale could have survived no other
method.

The ultimate object of science is foresight. It
may fairly be asked, therefore, supposing these
speculations to have any scientific justification, what
light do they throw on the future? It would be
foolish to suppose that speculations so general can
yield, in forecasting the future, a precision which
they do not pretend to possess. Keeping, however, to the level of very general inference, two
observations may be hazarded.

First, the ultimate destiny of Germany cannot
be regarded as very much in doubt. If we are
content to look beyond this war, however it may
issue, and take in a longer stretch of time, we can
say with quite a reasonable degree of assurance
that Germanic power, of the type we know and fear
to-day, is impermanent. Germany has left the path
of natural evolution, or rather, perhaps, has never
found it. Unless, therefore, her civilization undergoes a radical change, and comes to be founded on
a different series of instinctive impulses, it will
disappear from the earth. All the advantages she
has derived from conscious direction and organization will not avail to change her fate, because
conscious direction is potent only when it works
hand in hand with Nature, and its first task—which
the directors of Germany have neglected—is to find
out the path which man must follow.

Secondly, a word may be ventured about the
war in so far as the consideration of Germany alone
can guide us. As I have tried to show, her morale
is more rigidly conditioned than that of her
opponents. They have merely to maintain their
resistance, to do which they have certain psychological advantages, and they must win. She must
continue aggressive efforts, and if these can be held
by her enemies—not more—she must go on galvan-
izing her weary nerves until they fail to respond. I
am not for a moment venturing to suppose myself

13

competent to give the slightest hint upon the conduct of the war ; I am merely pointing out what I regard as a psychological fact. Whether it has any practical military value is not in my province to decide.

If one claimed the liberty of all free men, to have over and above considered judgment a real guess, one would be inclined to venture the opinion that, however well things go with the enemies of Germany, there will not be much fighting on German soil.

The proposition that the strength and weakness of Germany are rigidly conditioned by definite and ascertainable psychological necessities is, if it is valid, chiefly of interest to the strategist and those who are responsible for the general lines of the campaign against her. We may well, however, ask whether psychological principle yields any hint of guidance in the solution of the further and equally important problem of how her enemies are to secure and render permanent the fruits of the victory upon which they are resolved.

This problem has already been the subject of a good deal of controversy, which is likely to increase as the matter comes more and more into the field of practical affairs.

Two types of solution have been expounded which, apart from what inessential agreement they may show in demanding the resurrection of such small nations as Germany has been able to assassinate, differ profoundly in the treatment they propose for the actual enemy herself. Both profess to be based upon the desire for a really permanent peace, and the establishment of a truly stable equilibrium between the antagonists. It is upon the means by which this result is to be secured that differences arise.

The official solution, and that almost universally accepted by the bulk of the people, insists that the

" military domination of Prussia," " German militar-
ism," or the " German military system " as it is
variously phrased, must be wholly and finally
destroyed. This doctrine has received many inter-
pretations. In spite, however, of criticism by moder-
ates on the one hand and by unpractically ferocious
root-and-branch men on the other, it seems to
remain—significantly enough—an expression of
policy which the common man feels for the time to
be adequate.

The most considerable criticism has come from
the small class of accomplished and intellectual
writers who from their pacifist and " international "
tendencies have to some extent been accused, no
doubt falsely, of being pro-German in the sense
of anti-English. The complaint of this school
against the official declaration of policy is, that it
does not disclose a sufficiently definite object or the
means by which this object is to be attained. We
are told that as a nation we do not know what we
are fighting for, and, what amounts to the same
thing, that we cannot attain the object we profess
to pursue by the exercise of military force however drastically it may be applied. We are warned
that we should seek a " reasonable " peace and
one which by its moderation would have an
educative effect upon the German people, that to
crush and especially in any way to dismember the
German Empire would confirm its people in their
belief that this war is a war of aggression by
envious neighbours, and make revenge a national
aspiration.

Such criticism has not always been very effectually
answered, and the generally current feeling has
proved disconcertingly inarticulate in the presence
of its agile and well-equipped opponents. Indeed,
upon the ordinary assumptions of political debate,
it is doubtful whether any quite satisfactory answer

can be produced. It is just, however, these very assumptions which must be abandoned and replaced by more appropriate psychological principles when we are trying to obtain light upon the relations of two peoples of profoundly different social type and instinctive reaction. The common man seems to be dimly aware of this difference though he cannot define it ; the intellectual of what, for want of a better term, I may call the pacifist type in all its various grades, proceeds upon the assumption that no such difference exists. Much as one must respect the courage and capacity of many of these latter, one cannot but recognize that their conceptions, however logical and however ingenious, lack the invigorating contact with reality which the instinctive feelings of the common man have not altogether failed to attain.

Let us now consider what guidance in the solution of the problem can be got from a consideration of the peculiarities of the social type which the Germans of the present day, so characteristically present.

Regarded from this point of view, the war is seen to be directed against a social type which, when endowed with the technical resources of modern civilization, is, and must continue to be, a dangerous anachronism. A people of the aggressive social habit can never be in a state of stable equilibrium with its neighbours. The constitution of its society presents a rigid barrier to smooth and continuous internal integration ; its energy, therefore, must be occupied upon essentially, though not always superficially, external objects, and its history will necessarily be made up of alternating periods of aggression and periods of preparation. Such a people has no conception of the benign use of power. It must regard war as an end in itself, as the summit of its national activities, as the recurring apogee of its secular orbit ; it must regard peace as a necessary and somewhat irksome preparation for war in which it may savour reminiscently the joys of conquest by dragooning its new territories and drastically imposing upon them its national type. This instinctive insistence upon uniformity makes every conquest by such a people an impoverishment of the human race, and makes the resistance of such aggression an elementary human duty.

In every particular Germany has proved true to her social type, and every detail of her history for the last fifty years betrays the lupine quality, of her ideals and her morals.

We have seen that in all gregarious animals the social instinct must follow one of three principal types, each of which will produce a herd having special activities and reactions. The major units of the human species appear limited to a similar number of categories, but it is probable that the perpetuation of a given type in a given herd is not chiefly a matter of heredity in the individual. The individual is gregarious by inheritance ; the type according to which his gregarious reactions are manifested is not inherited, but will depend upon the form current in the herd to which he belongs, and handed down in it from generation to generation. Thus it has happened that nations have been able in the course of their history to pass from the aggressive to the socialized type. The change has perhaps been rendered possible by the existence of class segregation of a not too rigid kind, and has doubtless depended upon a progressive intercommunication and the consequently, developing altruism. The extremely rigid Prussian social system seems clearly to be associated with the persistence of the aggressive form of society.

In considering the permanent deliverance of Europe from the elements in Germany for which

there can be no possible toleration, we therefore
have not to deal with characters which must be
regarded as inherited in the biological sense. We
have to deal rather with a group of reactions which,
while owing their unity, coherence, and power to
the inherited qualities of the gregarious mind, owe
their perpetuation to organized State suggestion, to
tradition, and to their past success as a national
method.

There can be no doubt that the success of the
German Empire has consolidated the hold of the
aggressive social type upon its people, and has
guarded it from the eroding effects of increasing
communication with other peoples and knowledge
of the world. As I have already tried to show,
the moral power of such peoples is intimately
associated with the continuance of aggression and
of success. The German Empire has had no experience of failure, and for this reason has been able
to maintain its ideals and aspirations untouched by
modern influences. It needs no psychological insight
to foretell that if the result of this war can be in
any way regarded as a success for Germany, she
will be thereby confirmed in her present ideals,
however great her sufferings may have been, and
however complete her exhaustion. It must be remembered that this type of people is capable of
interpreting facts in accordance with its prejudices
to an almost incredible extent, as we have seen
time and again in the course of the war. The
proof that the aggressive national type is intolerable in modern Europe, if it can be afforded by
force of arms, must therefore be made very plain,
or it will have no value as a lesson. Proof of failure
adequate to convince a people of the socialized type
might be quite inadequate to convince a people
of the lupine type in whom, from the nature of the
case, mental resistiveness is so much more impene-

trable. This is the psychological fact of which
the statesmen of Europe will have to be, above
all things, aware when questions of peace come
seriously to be discussed, for otherwise they will
risk the loss of all the blood and treasure which
have been expended without any corresponding gain
for civilization.

We have been warned that to " humiliate " Germany will merely be to set her upon the preparation
of vengeance, and to confirm her belief in the
supreme value of military strength. This opinion
affects to be based on a knowledge of human nature,
but its pretensions are not very well founded. The
passion of revenge is habitually over-estimated as
a motive—possibly through the influence of the
novelists and playwrights to whom it is so useful.
When we examine man's behaviour objectively we
find that revenge, however deathless a passion it
is vowed to be at emotional moments, is in actual
life constantly having to give way to more urgent
and more recent needs and feelings. Between
nations there is no reason to suppose that it has
any more reality as a motive of policy, though it
perhaps has slightly more value as a consolatory
pose.

It is curious that the naïve over-estimation of
the revenge ideal should have been uninfluenced by
so obvious an example as the relations of France
and Germany. In 1870 the former was " humili-
ated " with brutal completeness and every element
of insult. She talked of revenge, as she could
scarcely fail to do, but she soon showed that her
grasp on reality was too firm to allow her policy
to be moved by that childish passion. Characteristically, it was the victorious aggressor who believed
in her longing for revenge, and who at length
attacked her again.

A psychological hint of great value may be obtained from our knowledge of those animals whose gregariousness, like that of the Germans, is of the aggressive type. When it is thought necessary to correct a dog by corporal measures, it is found that the best effect is got by what is rather callously called a " sound " thrashing. The animal must be left in no doubt as to who is the master, and his punishment must not be diluted by hesitation, nervousness, or compunction on the part of the punisher. The experience then becomes one from which the dog is capable of learning, and if the sense of mastery conveyed to him is unmistakable, he can assimilate the lesson without reservation or the desire for revenge. However repulsive the idea may be to creatures of the socialized type, no sentimentalism and no pacifist theorizing can conceal the fact that the respect of a dog can be won by violence. If there is any truth in the view I have expressed that the moral reactions of Germany follow the gregarious type which is illustrated by the wolf and the dog, it follows that her respect is to be won by a thorough and drastic beating, and it is just that elementary respect for other nations, of which she is now entirely free, which it is the duty of Europe to teach her. If she is allowed to escape under conditions which in any way can be sophisticated into a victory, or, at any rate, not a defeat, she will continue to hate us as she continued to hate her victim France.

To the politician, devoted as he necessarily is to the exclusively human point of view, it may seem fantastic and scandalous to look for help in international policy to the conduct of dogs. The gulf between the two fields is not perhaps so impassably profound as he would like to think, but, however that may be, the analogy I have drawn is not unsupported by evidence of a more respectable kind.

The susceptibility of the individual German to a harsh and even brutally enforced discipline is well known. The common soldier submits to be beaten by his sergeant, and is the better soldier for it ; both submit to the bullying of their officer apparently also with profit ; the common student is scarcely less completely subject to his professor, and becomes thereby a model of scientific excellence ; the common citizen submits to the commands of his superiors, however unreasonably conceived and insultingly conveyed, and becomes a model of disciplined behaviour ; finally the head of the State, combining the most drastic methods of the sergeant, the professor, and the official, wins not merely a slavish respect, but a veritable apotheosis.

Germany has shown unmistakably the way to her heart ; it is for Europe to take it.

England against Germany—England.

It is one of the most impressive facts about the war, that while Germany is the very type of a perfected aggressive herd, England is perhaps the most complete example of a socialized herd. Corresponding with this biological difference is the striking difference in their history. Germany has modelled her soul upon the wolf's, and has rushed through the possibilities of her archetype in fifty feverish years of development ; already she is a finished product, her moral ideal is fulfilled and leaves her nothing to strive for except the imposition of it upon the world. England has taken as her model the bee, and still lags infinitely far behind the fulfilment of her ideal. In the unbroken security of her land, for near a thousand years, she has leisurely, perhaps lazily, and with infinite slowness, pursued her path towards a social integration of an ever closer and deeper kind. She has stolidly, even stupidly, and always in a grossly practical spirit, held herself to the task of shaping a society in which free men could live and yet be citizens. She has had no theory of herself, no consciousness of her destiny, no will to power. She has had almost no national heroes, and has always been constitutionally frigid to her great men, grudging them the material for their experimentations on her people, indifferent to their expositions of her duty and her imperial destiny, granting them a chance to die for her with no more encouragement than an impatient sigh. She has allowed an empire to be won for her by her restless younger sons, has shown no gratification in their conquests, and so far from thrilling with the exultation of the conqueror, has always at the earliest moment set her new dominions at work upon the problem in which her wholly unromantic absorption has never relaxed. And after a thousand years she seems as far as ever from her goal. Her society is irregular, disorganized, inco-ordinate, split into classes at war with one another, weighted at one end with poverty, squalor, ignorance, and disease, weighted at the other end by ignorance, prejudice, and corpulent self-satisfaction. Nevertheless, her patience is no more shaken by what she is lectured upon as failure than was her composure by what she was assured was imperial success. She is no less bound by her fate than is Germany, and must continue her path until she reaches its infinitely remoter goal. Nations may model themselves on her expedients, and found the architecture of their liberty on the tabernacles she has set up by the wayside to rest in for a night—she will continue on her road unconscious of herself or her greatness, absent-mindedly polite to genius, pleasantly tickled by prophets with very loud voices, but apt to go to sleep under

sermons, too awkward to boast or bluster, too
composed to seem strong, too dull to be flattered,
too patient to be flurried, and withal inflexibly
practical and indifferent to dreams.

No more perfect illustration of the characteristics
of the two nations could be found than their attitude
before the war. England the empiric, dimly conscious of trouble, was puzzled, restless, and uneasy,
in the face of a problem she was threatened with
some day having to study ; Germany the theorist,
cool, " objective," conscious of herself, was convinced there was no problem at all.

In studying the mind of England in the spirit of
the biological psychologist, it is necessary to keep
in mind the society of the bee, just as in studying
the German mind it was necessary to keep in mind
the society of the wolf.

One of the most striking phenomena which
observers of the bee have noticed is the absence of
any obvious means of direction or government in
the hive. The queen seems to be valued merely,
for her functions, which are in no way directive.
Decisions of policy of the greatest moment appear,
as far as we can detect, to arise spontaneously among
the workers, and whether the future is to prove
them right or wrong, are carried out without protest
or disagreement. This capacity for unanimous
decisions is obviously connected with the limited
mental development of the individual, as is shown
by the fact that in man it is very much more feeble.
In spite of this, the unanimity of the hive is wonderfully effective and surprisingly successful. Specu-
lators upon the physiology and psychology of bees
have been forced—very tentatively of course—to
imagine that creatures living in such intensely close
communion are able to communicate to one another,
and, as it were, to a common stock, such extremely

simple conceptions as they can be supposed to
entertain, and produce, so to say, a communal mind
which comes to have, at any rate in times of crisis,
a quasi-independent existence. The conception is
difficult to express in concrete terms, and even to
grasp in more than an occasional intuitive flash.
Whether we are to entertain such a conception or
are to reject it, the fact remains that societies of
a very closely communal habit are apt to give the
appearance of being ruled by a kind of common
mind—a veritable spirit of the hive—although no
trace of any directive apparatus can be detected.

A close study of England gives the impression of
some agency comparable with a " spirit of the hive "
being at work within it. The impression is not
perhaps to be taken as altogether fantastic, when we
remember how her insular station and her long
history have forced upon her a physical seclusion
and unity resembling, though of course far less
complete than, that of the hive. I am of course not
unaware that disquisitions upon the national spirit
are very familiar to us. These, however, are so
loosely conceived, so much concerned with purely
conventional personifications of quite imaginary
qualities, that I cannot regard them as referring
to the phenomenon I am trying to describe.

The conception in my mind is that of an old and
isolated people, developing, by the slow mingling
and attrition of their ideas, and needs, and impulses,
a certain deeply lying unity which becomes a kind
of " instinct " for national life, and gives to national
policy, without the conscious knowledge of any
individual citizen, without the direction of statesmen,
and perhaps in spite of them all, a continuity of
trend, and even an intelligence, by which events may
be influenced in a profoundly important way.

The making of some such assumption, helped as
it is by the analogy of the bee, seems to be neces-

sary when we consider at all objectively the history of England and her Empire. She has done so much without any leading, so much in spite of her ostensible leaders, so often a great policy or a successful stroke has been apparently accidental. So much of her work that seemed, while it was doing, to be local and narrow in conception and motive displays at a distance evidences of design on the great scale. Her contests with Philip of Spain, with Louis XIV, with Napoleon, and the foundation of her Colonial Empire, would seem to be the grandiose conceptions of some supreme genius did we not know how they were undertaken and in what spirit pursued.

It appears, then, that England has something with which to retort upon the conscious direction to which Germany owes so much of her strength. Among the number of embattled principles and counter principles which this war has brought into the field, we must include as not the least interesting the duel between conscious national direction on the one side and unconscious national will and knowledge on the other.

It is quite outside my province to touch upon the diplomatic events which led up to the war. They seem to me to be irrelevant to the biological type of analysis we are trying to pursue. There can be no doubt at all that the ordinary consciousness of the vast majority of citizens of this country was intensely averse from the idea of war. Those who were in general bellicose were for the moment decidedly out of influence. Can we suppose, however, that the deep, still spirit of the hive that whispers unrecognized in us all had failed to note that strange, gesticulating object across the North Sea? In its vast, simple memory would come up other objects that had gone on like that. It would remember a mailed fist that had been flourished across the Bay of Biscay three hundred years ago, a little man in shining armour who had strutted threateningly on the other shore of the Channel, and the other little man who had stood there among his armies, and rattled his sabre in the scabbard. It had marked them all down in their time, and it remembered the old vocabulary. It would turn wearily and a little impatiently to this new portent over the North Sea. . . . Wise with the experience of a thousand years, it would know when to strike.

Such deeply buried combined national impulses as we are here glancing at are far removed from the influence of pacifist or jingo. Any attempt to define them must be a matter of guesswork and groping, in which the element of speculation is far in excess of the element of ascertained fact. It seems, however, that, as in the case of the bee, they concern chiefly actual decisions of crucial matters of policy. To put this suggestion in another form, we might say the spirit of the people makes the great wars, but it leaves the statesman to conduct them. It may make, therefore, a decision of incredible profundity, launch the people on the necessary course at the necessary moment, and then leave them to flounder through the difficulties of their journey as best they can. Herein is the contrast it presents with the German resource of conscious direction—superficial, apt to blunder in all the larger, deeper matters of human nature, but constant, alert, and ingenious in making immediate use of every available means and penetrating every department of activity.

During the conduct of war it is only in the simplest, broadest matters that the spirit of the people can bring its wisdom to bear. One of the most striking manifestations of it has, for example, been the way in which it has shown a knowledge that the war would be long and hard. The bad news has been, in general, received without complaint, reproach, or agitation, the good news, such as it has been, with a resolute determination not to exult or rejoice. That so many months of a deadly war have produced no *popular* expression of exultation or dismay, is a substantial evidence of moral power, and not the less impressive for being so plainly, the work of the common man himself.

Such manifestations of the spirit of the people are rare, and meet with very little encouragement from those who have access to the public. It is astonishing how absent the gift of interpretation seems to be. A few, a very few, stand out as being able to catch those whispers of immemorial wisdom; many, seem to be occupied in confusing them with a harsh and discordant clamour of speech.

If we are correct in our analogy of the bee and the wolf, England has one great moral advantage over Germany, namely, that there is in the structure of her society no inherent obstacle to perfect unity, among her people. The utmost unity Germany can compass is that of the aggressive type, which brings with it a harsh, non-altruistic relation among individuals, and can yield its full moral value only, during the maintenance of successful attack. England, on the other hand, having followed the socialized type of gregariousness, is free to integrate her society to an indefinite extent. The development of the altruistic relation among her individuals lies in her natural path. Her system of social segregation is not necessarily a rigid one, and if she can bring about an adequate acceleration of the perfectly natural consolidation towards which she is, and has slowly been, tending, she will attain access to a store of moral power literally inexhaustible, and will reach a moral cohesion which no hardship can shake, and an endurance which no power on earth can overcome.

These are no figures of speech, but plain biological fact, capable of immediate practical application and yielding an immediate result. It must be admitted that she has made little progress towards this consummation since the beginning of the war. Leaders, including not only governing politicians but also those who in any, way have access to public notice, tend to enjoin a merely conventional unity, which is almost functionless in the promotion of moral strength. It is not much more than an agreement to say we are united ; it produces no true unity of spirit and no power in the individual to deny himself the indulgence of his egoistic impulses in action and in speech, and is therefore as irritating as it is useless. It is unfortunate that the education and circumstances of many public men deny them any opportunity of learning the very elementary principles which are necessary for the development of a nation's moral resources. Occasionally one or another catches an intuitive glimpse of some fragment of the required knowledge, but never enough to enable him to develop any effective influence. For the most part their impulses are as likely to be destructive of the desired effect as favourable to it. In the past England's wars have always been conducted in an atmosphere of disunion, of acrimony, and of criticism designed to embarrass the Government rather than, as it professes, to strengthen the country. It is a testimony to the moral sturdiness of the people, and to the power and subtlety of the spirit of the hive, that success has been possible in such conditions. When one remembers how England has flourished on domestic discord in criti-

cal times, one is tempted to believe that she derives
some mysterious power from such a state, and that
the abolition of discord might not be for her the
advantageous change it appears so evidently to be.
Consideration, however, must show that this hypothesis is inadmissible, and that England has won
through on these occasions in spite of the handicap
discord has put upon her.   In the present war,
tough and hard as is her moral fibre, she will need
every element of her power to avoid the weariness
and enfeeblement that will otherwise come upon
her before her task is done.

Throughout the months of warfare that have
already passed no evidence has become public of
any recognition that the moral power of a nation
depends upon causes which can be identified, formulated, and controlled.   It seems to be unknown
that that domination of egoistic impulses by social
impulses which we call a satisfactory morale is
capable of direct cultivation as such, that by it the
resources of the nation are made completely available to the nation's leaders, that without it every
demand upon the citizen is liable to be grudgingly
met or altogether repudiated.

We are told by physicians that uninstructed
patients are apt to insist upon the relief of their
symptoms, and to care nothing for the cure of
their diseases, that a man will demand a bottle of
medicine to stop the pain of an ulcer in his stomach,
but will refuse to allow the examination that would
establish the nature of his disease.   The statesman
embarrassed by the manifestations of an imperfect
morale seems to incline to a similar method.   When
he finds he cannot get soldiers at the necessary rate,
he would invent a remedy for that particular
symptom.   When he has difficulties in getting one
or another industrial class to suspend its charters
in the interests of the State, he must have a new

and special nostrum for that. When he would relax the caution of the capitalist or restrain the wastefulness of the self-indulgent, again other remedies must be found. And so he passes from crisis to crisis, never knowing from moment to moment what trouble will break out next, harassed, it is to be supposed, by the doubt whether his stock of potions and pills will hold out, and how long their very moderate efficiency will continue.

None of these troubles is a disease in itself; all are evidences of an imperfect national morale, and any attempt to deal with them that does not reach their common cause will necessarily, therefore be unsatisfactory and impermanent.

The sole basis of a satisfactory morale in a people of the social type that obtains in England is a true national unity, which is therefore the singular and complete remedy for all the civil difficulties incident upon a great and dangerous war.

It is impossible to form any guess whether England will keep to her traditional methods or will depart so far from them as to take a bold and comprehensive view of her present and her growing moral needs. A carefully conceived and daringly carried out organization of a real national unity would have no great difficulty in a country so rich in practical genius; it would make an end once for all of every internal difficulty of the State, and would convert the nation into an engine of war which nothing could resist.

The more probable and the characteristic event will be a mere continuation in the old way. It will exemplify our usual and often admirable enough contempt for theoretical considerations and dreams, our want of interest in knowledge and foresight, our willingness to take any risk rather than endure the horrid pains of thought.

When we remember how costly is our traditional method, how long and painful it makes the way, how doubtful it even makes the goal, it is impossible for the most philosophic to restrain a sigh for the needless suffering it entails, and a thrill of alarm for the dangers it gives our path, the darkness around us and ahead, the unimaginable end.

To the student, the end of the chapter is a chance to turn from the study of detail and allow his mind to range through a larger atmosphere and over a longer sequence. Closing our small chapter, we also may look at large over the great expanse of the biological series in whose illimitable panorama the war that covers our nearer skies with its blood-red cloud is no bigger than a pin point. As we contemplate in imagination the first minute spot of living jelly that crept and hungered in the mud, we can see the interplay of its necessities and its powers already pushing it along the path at the end of which we stand. Inherent in the dot of magic substance that was no longer mere carbon, hydrogen, oxygen, nitrogen, sulphur, and a little phosphorus, was the capacity to combine with its fellows and to profit by the fellowship, however loose. In the slow process of time combination brought freedom which, just like ours, was freedom to vary and, varying, to specialize. So in time great States of cells grew up, their individual citizen cells specialized to the finest pitch, perfect in communion with one another, co-ordinate in all their activities, incorporated with the State.

These new and splendid organizations, by the very fact of giving freedom to the individual cells, had lost it themselves. Still, they retained their capacity for combination, and where the need of

freedom was greatest they found it again in a new
combination on a bigger scale. Thus again was
obtained freedom to vary, to specialize, to react.
Over the world fellowships of all grades and almost
all types of creatures sprang up. Specialization,
communion, co-ordination again appeared on the new
plane. It was as if Nature, to protect her children
against herself, was trying to crowd as much living
matter into one unit as she could. She had failed
with her giant lizards, with the mammoth and the
mastodon. She would try a new method which
should dispense with gross physical aggregations,
but should minister to the same needs and afford the
same powers. The body should be left free, the
mind alone should be incorporated in the new unit.
The non-material nexus proved as efficient as the
physical one had been. The flock, the herd, the
pack, the swarm, new creatures all, flourished and
ranged the world. Their power depended on the
capacity for intercommunication amongst their
members and expanded until the limits of this were
reached. As long as intercommunication was limited
the full possibilities of the new experiment were
concealed, but at length appeared a creature in
whom this capacity could develop indefinitely. At
once a power of a new magnitude was manifest.
Puny as were his individuals, man's capacity for
communication soon made him master of the world.
The very quality, however, which gave him success
introduced a new complication of his fate. His
brain power allowed him to speak and understand
and so to communicate and combine more effectively
than any other animal ; his brain power gave him
individuality and egoism, and the possibility of
varied reaction which enabled him to obey the voice
of instinct after the fashion of his own heart. All
combination therefore was irregular, inco-ordinate,
and only very slowly progressive. He has even at

times wandered into blind paths where the possibility of progressive combination is lost.

Nevertheless the needs and capacities that were at work in the primeval amœba are at work in him. In his very flesh and bones is the impulse towards closer and closer union in larger and larger fellowships. To-day he is fighting his way towards that goal, fighting for the perfect unit which Nature has so long foreshadowed, in which there shall be a complete communion of its members, unobstructed by egoism or hatred, by harshness or arrogance or the wolfish lust for blood. That perfect unit will be a new creature, recognizable as a single entity, ; to its million-minded power and knowledge no barrier will be insurmountable, no gulf impassable, no task too great.

POSTSCRIPT OF 1919

Prejudice in Time of War.

WITH the exception of the two preliminary essays, the foregoing chapters were written in the autumn of 1915. As the chief purpose of the book was to expound the conception that psychology is a science practically useful in actual affairs, it was inevitable that a great deal of the exemplary matter by which it was attempted to illustrate the theoretical discussion should be related to the war of 1914–1918. Rich, however, as this subject was in material with which to illustrate a psychological inquiry, it presented also the great difficulty of being surrounded and permeated by prejudices of the most deeply impassioned kind, prejudices, moreover, in one direction or another from which no inhabitant of one of the belligerent countries could have the least expectation of being free. To yield to the temptation offered by the psychological richness of war themes might thus be to sacrifice the detachment of mind and coolness of judgment without which scientific investigation is impossible. It had to be admitted, in fact, that there were strong grounds for such epistemological pessimism, and it will perhaps be useful in a broad way to define some of these here.

In normal times a modern nation is made up of a society in which no regard is paid to moral unity, and in which therefore common feeling is to

a great extent unorganized and inco-ordinate. In
such a society, the individual citizen cannot derive
from the nation as a whole the full satisfaction
of the needs special to him as a gregarious animal.
The national feeling he experiences when at home
among his fellows is too vague and remote to
call forth the sense of moral vigour and security
that his nature demands. As has already been
pointed out [1] the necessary consequence is the
segregation of society into innumerable minor
groups, each constituting in itself a small herd,
and dispensing to its members the moral energy
that in a fully organized society would come from
the nation as a whole. Of such minor herds some
are much more distinct from the common body than
others. Some engage a part only of the life of
their members, so that the individual citizen may
belong to a number of groups and derive such
moral energy as he possesses from a variety of
sources. Thus in a fully segregated society in
time of peace the moral support of the citizen
comes from his social class and his immediate circle,
his professional associations, his church, his chapel,
his trade union and his clubs, rather than directly
from the nation in which he is a unit. Indeed,
so far from looking to the nation at large for the
fulfilment of its natural function of providing "all
hope, all sustainment, all reward," he is apt to regard
it as embodied by the tax-gatherer, the policeman,
and the bureaucrat, at its best remote and indifferent,
at its worst hostile and oppressive.

The more distinct of these intra-national groups
may not only be very fully isolated from the common
body, but may be the seat of an actual corporate
hostility to it, or rather to the aggregated minor
groups which have come officially to represent it.
When war breaks upon a society thus constituted

[1] Pp. 137, 138 *supra*.

the intense stimulation of herd instinct that results
tends to break down the moral restrictions set up
by segregation, to throw back the individual citizen
on to the nation at large for the satisfaction of
his moral needs, and to replace class feeling by
national feeling. The apprehended danger of the
given war is the measure of the completeness with
which occurs such a solution of minor groups into
the national body. The extent of such solution
and the consequently increased homogeneity it
effects in the nation will determine the extent to
which national feeling develops, the degree to which
it approaches unanimity, and consequently the vigour
with which the war is defended and conducted.
If a minor group has already developed a certain
hostility to the common body and resists the solvent
effect of the outbreak of war, it becomes a potential
source of anti-national feeling and of opposition to the
national policy. Surrounded as it necessarily will be
by an atmosphere of hostility, its character as a herd
becomes hardened and invigorated, and it can endow
its members with all the gifts of moral vigour and
resistiveness a herd can give. Thus we may say,
that in a country at war *every* citizen is exposed
to the extremely powerful stimulation of herd instinct
characteristic of that state. In the individual who
follows in feeling the general body of his fellows,
and in him who belongs to a dissentient minority,
the reactions peculiar to the gregarious animal will
be energetically manifested. Of such reactions, that
which interests us particularly at the moment is
the moulding of opinion in accordance with instinctive pressure, and we arrive at the conclusion that
our citizen of the majority is no more—if no less—
liable to the distortion of opinion than our citizen
of the minority. Whence we conclude that in a
country at war *all* opinion is necessarily more or
less subject to prejudice, and that this liability to

bias is a herd mechanism, and owes its vigour to
that potent instinct.

It is undoubtedly depressing to have to recognize
this universality of prejudice and to have to abandon
the opinion sometimes held that the characteristics
of herd belief are limited to the judgments of the
vulgar. The selectness of a minority in no way
guarantees it against the fallacies of the mob. A
minority sufficiently unpopular is, in a sense, a mob
in which smallness is compensated for by density.
The moral vigour and fortitude which unpopular
minorities enjoy are evidences of herd instinct in
vigorous action ; the less admirable liability to
prejudice being a part of the same instinctive
process is a necessary accompaniment. We may
lay it down, then, as fundamental that all opinion
among the members of a nation at war is liable
to prejudice, and when we remember with what
vehemence such opinion is pronounced and with
what fortitude it is defended we may regard as
at least highly probable that such opinion always
actually is prejudiced—rests, that is to say, on
instinct rather than reason. Now, it is common
knowledge that in the present state of society
opinion in a given country is always divided as to
the justice of an actual war. All of it sharing the
common characteristic of war opinion in being
prejudiced, some will pronounce more or less clearly
that the war is just and necessary, some will
pronounce more or less clearly against that view ;
there will be a division into what we may call
pro-national and anti-national currents of opinion,
each accompanied respectively by its counterpart
of what we may call anti-hostile and pro-hostile
opinion. It is a significant fact that the relative
development of pro-national and anti-national
feeling varies according to the degree in which
the given war is apprehended as dangerous. A

war apprehended as dangerous produces a more
complete solution of the minor herds of society
into the common body than does a war not so
regarded ; in consequence there is a nearer
approach to homogeneity, and pro-national opinion
is far in excess of anti-national opinion, which, if
recognizable, is confined to insignificant minorities.
A war regarded as not dangerous produces a less
complete solution in the common body, a less degree
of homogeneity, and allows anti-national opinion,
that is, doubt of the justice of the war and opposition to the national policy, to develop on a large
scale. These phenomena have been clearly visible
in the history of recent wars. The South African
War of 1899-1902 was not apprehended as
dangerous in this country, and in consequence,
though pro-national opinion prevailed among the
majority, anti-national opinion was current in a
large and respectable minority. The war of 1914-
1918, regarded from the first as of the greatest
gravity, gave to pro-national opinion an enormous
preponderance, and restricted anti-national opinion
within very narrow limits. The Russo-Japanese
War provided an excellent double illustration of
these mechanisms. On the Russian side regarded as
not dangerous, it left national opinion greatly
divided, and made the conduct of the war confused
and languid ; on the Japanese side apprehended
as highly dangerous, it produced an enormous preponderance of pro-national opinion, and made the
conduct of the war correspondingly vigorous. In
the Franco-Prussian War of 1870-1871 a further
point is illustrated. The essential factor in the
stimulation of herd instinct by war is not the actual
danger of a given war, but the apprehended danger
of it. The Prussians were dangerous enough to
France, but were not generally regarded as such
by the French, and in consequence national homo ↴

'geneity did not develop as it did on a later occasion
in face of the same menace.

If pro-national and anti-national opinion, if belief
and doubt in the justice of a given war, vary in
relation to a single predominantly important psychological factor—the apprehended danger to the nation
of the war in question—it is obvious that the
ostensible and proclaimed grounds upon which such
opinion is founded are 'less decisive than is
commonly supposed. Finding, as we do, that
the way in which a people responds to the outbreak of war depends certainly in the main and
probably altogether on a condition not necessarily
dependent on the causes of the war, it is obvious
that the moral justifications which are usually,
regarded as so important in determining the people's
response are in fact comparatively, insignificant.
This conclusion agrees with the observed fact that
no nation at war ever lacks the conviction that its
cause is just. In the war of 1914-1918 each of
the belligerents was animated by, a passion of
certainty that its participation was unavoidable and
its purpose good and noble ; each side defended
its cause with arguments perfectly convincing and
unanswerable to itself and wholly, without effect on
the enemy. Such passion, such certitude, such
impenetrability were obviously products of something other than reason, and do not in themselves
and directly give us any information as to the
objective realities of the distribution of justice
between the two sides. The sense of rectitude is
in fact and manifestly, a product of mere belligerency,
and one which a nation at war may confidently,
expect to possess, no matter how nefarious its
objects may ultimately, appear to be in the eyes
of general justice. The fact that such a sense of
rectitude is a universal and inevitable accompaniment of war, and as strong in a predatory, and

criminal belligerent as in a generally pacific one,
gives us a convenient measure of the extent to
which prejudice must prevail in warfare.[1]

We thus arrive at the discouraging conclusion
that in a belligerent country all opinion in any
way connected with the war is subject to prejudice,
either pro-national or anti-national, and is very
likely in consequence to be of impaired validity.
Must we then conclude further that speculation upon
war themes is so liable to distortion that reasoned
judgments of any practical value are impossible?
Now, it is guidance in just such a difficulty as
this that a psychology having any pretensions to
be called practical may fairly be expected to yield,
and psychology does in fact provide certain broad
precautionary principles, which, although by no
means infallible guides, do profess to be able to
keep within bounds the disturbing effects of
prejudice on judgment and so render possible the
not wholly unprofitable discussion even of matters
the most deeply implicated by war-time passion.

First among such principles is the recognition of
the fact that prejudice does not display itself as
such to direct introspection. One who is being

[1] It is important that it should be quite clear that we have been
speaking here of the reaction of the general body of a nation to the
occurrence of war, and not of the reasons for which a given war was
undertaken. In England and in Germany the feeling of the people
that the late war was just and necessary was equally intense and
equally a direct consequence of the danger to the herd it represented.
It was therefore a non-rational instinctive response without reference
to objective justice in either case. Had the threat to the herd on
either side seemed less grave, opinion as to the justice of the war
would in that country have been correspondingly more divided. By
her calculated truculence in the years before the war Germany—
intending doubtless to intimidate a decaying people—had made it
certain that when the threat to this country did come it should be
apprehended at once as dangerous to the last degree, and had thus
herself organized the practical unanimity of her chief enemy. All
such reactions upon the outbreak of war are instinctively determined.
It is the burden of the statesman that his decision in a crisis in favour
of war *automatically* renders impossible *rational* confirmation by the
people.

influenced by prejudice will never be able to detect
his biassed judgments by an apparent defect in
their plausibility or by any characteristic logical
weakness.   Agreement or disagreement with common opinion will as such be no help, since prejudice
infests minorities no less than majorities.   To
suppose that when one has admitted the liability
to prejudice one can free oneself from it by a
direct voluntary effort is a common belief and an
entirely fallacious one.   Such a task is far beyond
the powers of the most fully instructed mind, and
is not likely to be undertaken except by those who
have least chance of success.   Prejudice, in fact,
is for the individual like the ether of the physicist,
infinitely pervasive and potent, but insusceptible of
direct detection ; its presence is to be assumed as
general, but it escapes before immediate search by
introspection as the ether eludes the balance and the
test-tube.

    Secondly, it is possible for the investigator,
having admitted the existence of prejudice as a
condition of thought, to recognize the general direction of its action in his own mind, to recognize,
that is to say, whether the tone of it is pro-national
or anti-national, and thus to obtain a certain orientation for his efforts to neutralize it.   Having frankly
recognized this general tendency in his thinking,
he will be able to do something towards correct-
ing it by making allowance for it in his conclusion
as a whole.   If his tendency of feeling is pro-
national, he will say to himself of any judgment
favourable to his country, " This is a conclusion
likely to have been influenced by prejudice, therefore for all the precautions I may have taken in
forming it, and whatever scientific care and caution
I may have used, in spite even of its agreeable
appearance of self-evident truth, I must regard its
validity as subject to some subtraction before it

can safely be made the basis for further speculation." If his tendency of feeling is anti-national,
he will have a similar task of attenuation to carry
out upon the conclusions unfavourable to his country,
that he may reach, and will be prudent to make
very drastic deductions in view of the supposed
immunity to prejudice with which minorities are
rather apt to assume the absence of vulgar approval
endows them.[1]

Finally, one who attempts to deal usefully with
matters in which strong feeling is inevitable will
do well, however thoroughly he may try to guard
himself from the effects of prejudice, to bring his
speculative conclusions into such form that they
are automatically tested by the progress of events.
Symmetry and internal consistency are unfortunately but too often accepted as evidences of objective
validity. That the items of a series of conclusions
fit into one another neatly and compose a system
logically sound and attractive to the intellect gives
us practically no information of their truth. For
this a frequently repeated contact with external
reality is necessary, and of such contacts the most
thoroughly satisfactory one is the power to foretell
the course of events. Foresight is the supreme

[1] It is perhaps of interest to note in passing that war-time opinion
and prejudice are characteristically pro-national and anti-national,
rather than anti-hostile and pro-hostile respectively. The impulse that
might have led an isolated German to defend the English at the
expense of his countrymen, or an isolated Englishman to defend the
Germans at the expense of his countrymen, was in its psychological
essence anti-national and animated by no love of the enemy ; it was
an instinctive revolt against his country, or rather the groups which
in the process of social segregation had come to represent it. Such
terms, therefore, as pro-German, and in another association pro-Boer,
though doubtless convenient implements of abuse, were inexactly
descriptive psychologically. " Anti-English " would have been more
just, but immensely less effective, as vituperation, for the prejudice it
was desired to decry was for the most part a hostility not to the nation,
but to its official embodiment. Probably, however, it was the very
element of injustice in the term pro-German that made it so
satisfactory a vehicle for exasperated feeling.

test of scientific validity, and the more a line of
argument is liable to deflection by non-rational
processes the more urgent is the need for it constantly to be put into forms which will allow its
capacity for foresight to be tested.   This was the
one great advantage amongst heavy handicaps
enjoyed by those who ventured into speculation
upon the international situation during the late war.
Events were moving so quickly from crisis to crisis
that it was possible for the psychologist to see
his judgments confirmed or corrected almost from
day to day, to see in the authentic fabric of reality
as it left the loom where he had had any kind
of foreknowledge, where he had been altogether
unprepared, and where he had failed in foresight
of some development that should have been within
his powers.

These three principles were those in accordance
with which it was attempted to conduct the discussion in this book of topics connected with the
war.   The writer was aware that neither was he
by nature or art immune to prejudice nor able
by some miracle of will power to lay down passion
when he took up the pen, and he admitted to
himself with what frankness he could command
the liability under which his conclusions would lie
of having been arrived at under the influence of
pro-national prejudice.   He hoped, however, that
a liberal allowance for the direction of his instinctive
bias and a grateful use of the diurnal corrective
of events might enable him to reach at any rate
some conclusions not altogether without a useful
tincture of validity.

It was possible, moreover, to put certain conclusions in a form which the development of the
war must confirm or disprove, and it may be interesting as a test of what was put forward as an
essay in an essentially practical psychology briefly,

to review these theoretical anticipations in the light of what actually has happened.

PSYCHOLOGICAL ANTICIPATIONS

The hypothesis was put forward that in the German people the reactions in which the herd instinct was manifesting itself were in accordance with the type to be seen in the predaceous social animals rather than the type which seems to be characteristic of modern Western civilizations. The next step was naturally to inquire whether the known characters of what we called aggressive gregarious- ness were able to account for the observed German peculiarities in reaction, and then to indicate what special features we might expect to appear in Germany under the developing stress of war if our hypothesis was sound.

Under the guidance of the hypothesis we found reason to believe that the morale of the German people was of a special kind, and essentially depen- dent for the remarkable vigour it then showed upon the possibility of continued successful aggression. This suggestion was borne out by the long series of offensive movements, increasing in weight and culminating in the spring of 1918, in the great attacks on which Germany broke herself. From the way in which these movements were announced and expected it became evident that during an enforced defensive the morale of Germany declined more rapidly than did that of her opponents. This was the essential confirmation of the psychological view we had put forward. Apart from all question of the strategic and merely military advantages of the offensive it was plain that Germany's moral need for the posture of attack was peculiarly and charac- teristically great. That she continually and con- vincedly—though perhaps injudiciously—declared the war to be one of defence only, that she had every-

thing to hope from disunion among her enemies
and little to fear from disunion among her friends,
that she was in assured possession of the most
important industrial districts of France, that she
had successfully brought into something like
equilibrium the resistance to the effects of the
blockade, and had proved like her animal proto-
types only to be more fierce and eager when she
was hungry—all of these strong objective reasons
for fighting a defensive delaying war were over-
whelmed by the crucially important requirement of
keeping the aggressive spirit strung up to the highest
pitch. The fighting spirit must be that of attack
and conquest, or it would break altogether. Our
hypothesis, therefore, enabled us to foresee that she
would have to go on torturing her declining frame
with one great effort after another until she had
fought herself to a standstill, and then, if her enemies
but just succeeded in holding her, her morale would
begin to decline, and to decline with terrible abrupt-
ness. We were even able to regard it as probable
that for all the talk of the war on the German
side being defensive only, for all the passionate
devotion to the Fatherland and the profound belief
in the sanctity of its frontiers, as a matter of cold
and dry reality, if it came to invasion, Germany
would not be defended by its inhabitants.

Another subject upon which the psychological
method of inquiry professed to yield some degree
of foresight was that—at that time—fruitful cause
of discussion, the objects for which the enemies
of Germany were fighting. Opinion at that time
was much ruled by the conception of a Germany,
gradually forced back upon and beyond her
frontiers, grim, implacable, irreconcilable, her
national spirit energized and made resilient by
humiliation, and clinging unconquerably to the
thought of a resurrection of her glory through the

15

faith of her sons. Under the influence of ideas of this romantic type, it was not always possible for opinion to be very precise upon what was to be made the object of the war in order to secure from Germany the safety of the civilizations opposed to hers. Psychologically, however, the moral condition of a beaten Germany seemed relatively easy to foretell. If the behaviour of other predaceous types was of any value as a guide, it was plain that a sound beating alone and in itself would produce all the effect that was needful. There could be no fear of the national morale being invigorated by defeat, but an enemy successfully invading Germany would necessarily find the one essential condition on which any subsequent security must be set up—the replacement of the aggressive and predaceous morale by complete moral collapse. These were the considerations that enabled one to say that considered psychologically the mere beating of Germany was the single object of the war. The completeness of the moral collapse which accompanied her beating seems to have been found remarkable and astonishing by very many, but can have been so only to those who had not interested themselves in the psychological aspects of the problem.

In stating, in 1915, these conclusions as to the social type and moral structure of Germany and in formulating the indications they seemed to give of the course of future events, it was necessary to make considerable deductions from the precision and detail with which one made one's small efforts at foresight in order to allow for the effects one's pro-national bias may have had in deflecting judgment. Enough, however, was stated definitely to enable the progress of events very clearly to confirm or disprove the conclusions arrived at. The not inconsiderable correspondences between the theoretical considerations and the actual development of events is perhaps enough to suggest that the method of speculation used has a certain validity.

In considering the psychological case of England we came to the conclusion that her morale depended on mechanisms different from those which were in action in Germany, and indicating that social development had in her followed a different type. We saw reason to suppose that this social type would be very much more resistant to discourage-ment and disaster than the aggressive type embodied in Germany, and that if England won the war it would be by virtue of the toughness of her nerve. The form of social organization represented by England was seen to contain a germ of strength not possessed by her enemy, an intensely resistant nucleus of moral power that underlay the immeasur-able waste and the inextricable confusion of her methods.   If the moral structure of Germany was of its kind fully developed, it was also primitive; if the moral structure of England was embryonic, it was also integrative and still capable of growth. If it was very obvious at that time how immensely responsive to intelligent and conscious direction the moral powers of England would have been, if it was obvious how largely such direction would have diminished the total cost of the war in time and suffering, if it was obvious that such direction would not, and almost certainly could not, be forthcoming, it was equally clear that the muddle, the mediocrity, the vociferation with which the war was being con-ducted were phenomena within the normal of the type and evolutionary stage of our society, and were not much more than froth on the surface of an invisible and unsounded stream.

If one had been content to estimate the moral condition of England at that time by the utterance of all ordinary organs of expression—public speeches, leading articles and so forth—one could scarcely have failed to reach the gloomiest conclusions. So common were ill-will, acrimony, suspicion and intrigue, so often was apparent self-possession mere languor, and apparent energy mere querulousness, so strong, in fact, were all the ordinary evidences of moral disintegration that an actual collapse might have seemed almost within sight. As a matter of fact, from the very necessities of her social type, in England the organs of public expression were characteristically not representative of the national mood ; probably far less than were those of Germany representative of the German mood. Thus it came about that the actual driving force—the will of the common man, as inflexible as it was inarticulate— remained intact behind all the ambiguous manifestations which went forth as the voice of England. This is the psychological secret of the socialized type of gregarious animal. As evolved in England to-day, this type cannot attain to the conscious direction of its destiny, and cannot submit to the fertilizing discipline of science ; it cannot select its agents or justly estimate their capacity, but it possesses the power of evolving under pressure a common purpose of great stability. Such a common purpose is necessarily simple, direct, and barely conscious ; high-flown imperialism and elaborate policies are altogether beyond its range, and it can scarcely accomplish an intellectual process more complex than the recognition of an enemy. The conviction that the hostility between England and Germany was absolute and irreconcilable, and the war a matter of national life and death, was just such a primitive judgment as could be arrived at, and it gave rise to a common purpose as stable as it was simple.[1]

[1] There can be little doubt that national consciousness with regard to the war was very much less developed in this country than in

The relatively complex national consciousness that is necessary to evolve a positive movement of national expansion or a definite policy of colonization and aggrandisement seems to be hostile to the development of a common purpose of the most powerful kind. Thus we find moral vigour and stability attaining their greatest strength in a nation that has no definite theory of its destiny, and that is content to allow confusion of thought and vagueness of aim to be common and even characteristic in its public life. In such a people national consciousness is of the most elementary kind, and only the simplest conceptions can be effectively apprehended by it. Negative judgments are in general simpler than positive ones, and the simplest of all, perhaps, is the identification of an enemy. The history of England seems to show with remarkable constancy that the national consciousness has been in its most effective action limited to those elementary conceptions which have been simple and broad enough to manifest themselves in a common purpose of great strength and tenacity. England has, in fact, been made by her enemies. Rightly or wrongly, Philip of Spain, Louis XIV, Napoleon, Germany, impressed themselves on the elementary consciousness of England as enemies, and excited in response a unity of purpose that was characteristically as immune from the effects of discouragement, disaster and fatigue as it was independent of reasoned political theory.

Germany. The theory of his country's purpose in the war was far less a matter of interest and speculation to the average Englishman than it was to the average German. The German was far more fully aware of the relation the situation bore to general politics and to history, and was much more preoccupied with the defence of his country's case by rational methods and accepted principles, and he displayed from the first great faith in the value of a propaganda which should appeal to reason. Clumsy and futile as so much of this intellectual effort was ultimately seen to be, it did show that the interest in national affairs was more conscious and elaborate, and stood from the intellectual point of view at a higher level than it did in England.

Each of these enemies, in contrast with England, had the definite consciousness of a more or less elaborate political aim, and some of them embodied principles or methods in advance of those which obtained in England in corresponding fields. Whatever loftiness of aim they had availed them no more than their respect for principle and the intellect, and they all came to regret the mostly inadvertent effect of their pretensions in exciting the hostility of a people capable of an essential moral cohesion. The power of England would seem to have resided almost exclusively in this capacity for developing under pressure a common purpose. The immense moral energy she has been able to put forth in a crisis has enabled her to inspire such leaders as she has needed for the moment, but she has been characteristically infertile in the production of true leaders who could impose themselves upon her efficiently. Thus among her great men, for one true leader, such as Oliver Cromwell, who failed, there have been a score of successful mouthpieces and instruments of her purpose, such as Pitt and Wellington. The vigour of her great moments has always been the product of moral unity induced by the pressure of a supposed enemy, and therefore it has always tended to die down when the danger has passed. As the greatness of her leaders has been less a product of their own genius than that of the moral stimulus which has reached them from the nation at large, when the stimulus has been withdrawn with the cessation of danger, these men have almost invariably come to appear in times of peace of a less dominating capacity than their performance during the stress of war might have indicated. The great wars of England have usually, then, been the affair of the common man ; he has supplied the impulse that has made and the moral vigour that has conducted

them, he has created and inspired his leaders and
has endowed his representatives in the field and
on the sea with their stern and enduring pugnacity.

These conclusions have been confirmed by the
way in which the war progressed and came to
an end.   The war became more and more fully a
contest of moral forces until it ended in the unique
event of a surrender practically unconditional that
was not preceded by a total physical defeat.
German morale proved throughout extremely sensitive to any suspension of the aggressive posture,
and showed the unsuitability of its type in modern
conditions by undergoing at the mere threat of
disaster a disintegration so absolute that it must
remain a classical and perfect example in the records
of psychology.   There can be no doubt that had
there been among her enemies the least understanding of her moral type and state, her collapse
could have been brought about with comparative
ease at a much earlier date.   English morale, on
the other hand, seemed actually to be invigorated
by defeat, and even remained untouched by the
more serious trials of uninspired and mediocre
direction, of ill-will, petty tyranny, and confusion.

The confrontation in war of two types of social
structure differing so radically and by such clearly
defined characters as did Germany and England
was, as has been already suggested, a remarkable
instance of statecraft being forced into a region of
very much greater reality than that in which it
usually operates.   The historical scale of events,
with its narrow range, its reckoning by dynasties and
parliaments, its judgments in terms of tribal censure
and approbation, was found momentarily to march
with the biological scale where events are measured
by the survival or extinction of species, where time
acquires a new meaning, and the individual man,

however conspicuous historically, takes on the insect-like sameness of his fellows. Here was an experiment set out in Nature's laboratory, and for the first time the issues were so narrowly focussed as to be within the apprehension of the very subjects of the research. The matter to be tested concerned the whole validity of gregariousness. Two types were confronted. In one the social habit had taken a form that limited the participation of the individual in the social unit ; a rigid segregation of the society made it impossible to admit the moral equality of its members, and resulted in the activities of the social instinct being available solely through leadership ; it was a led society where internal cohesion and integration were replaced by what we may call external cohesion—a migratory society, developing its highest manifestations of the herd when it was being successfully led. In the other type the social habit had tended, however slowly and incompletely, towards the unlimited participation of the individual in the social unit. The tendency of the society was towards integration and internal cohesion ; it was therefore unaggressive, refractory to leadership, and apt to develop its highest herd manifestations when threatened and attacked. The former enjoyed all the advantages of a led society. It was tractable, and its leaders could impose upon it a relative uniformity of outlook and a high standard of general training. The latter had no advantage save the potentiality—and it was little more—of unlimited internal cohesion. It was intractable to leadership, and in consequence knowledge and training were limited and extremely localized within it ; it had no approach to unity of outlook, and its interests were necessarily concentrated on its internal rather than its external relations.

If the former type proved the stronger, any progressive evolution of society, in a direction that promised the largest extension of human powers would become very improbable ; the internal cohesion of social units would have appeared to be subject to limits, and the most hopeful prospective solution of human difficulties would have vanished. Conceivably accidental factors might have decided the issue of the experiment and left the principle still in doubt. As it happened, every element of chance that intruded went against the type that ultimately proved the stronger, and in the final decision the moral element was so conspicuously more significant than the physical that the experiment has yielded a result which seems to be singularly conclusive and unexceptionable.[1]

The result of the experiment has been decisive, and it is still a possibility that the progressive integration of society will ultimately yield a medium in which the utmost needs of the individual and of the race will be reconciled and satisfied. Had the more primitive social type—the migratory, aggressive society of leadership and the pack—had this proved still the master of the less primitive socialized and integrative type, the ultimate outlook for the race would have indeed been black. This is by no means to deny that German civilization had a vigour, a respect for knowledge, and even a benignity within which comfortable life was possible. But it is to assert that it was a regression, a choice of the easy path, a surrender to the tamer platitudes of

[1] Anxiety has frequently been expressed since the armistice of November, 1918, as to whether Germany has properly assimilated the lesson of her defeat, and undergone the desired change of heart. In the face of such doubts it is well to remember that there is another conclusion about the assimilation of which there need be no anxiety. It is at any rate clearly proved that Germany's enemies were able to beat her in spite of all the disadvantages of exterior lines, divided counsels, divergent points of view and inadequate preparation. The prestige of invulnerability need never be allowed again to accumulate about a social group of the aggressive migratory type, and to sit like an incubus upon a terrorized world.

the spirit that no aggressive vigour could altogether mask. To live dangerously was supposed to be its ideal, but dread was the very atmosphere it breathed. Its armies could be thrown into hysterical convulsions by the thought of the *franc-tireur*, and the flesh of its leaders made to creep by such naïve and transpontine machinations as its enemies ambitiously called propaganda. The minds that could make bugbears out of such material were little likely to attempt or permit the life of arduous and desperate spiritual adventure that was in the mind of the philosopher when he called on his disciples to live dangerously.

This great experiment was conducted under the very eyes of humanity, and the conditions were unique in this that they would have permitted the effective intervention of the conscious human will. As it happened the evolution of society had not reached a stage at which an informed and scientific statecraft was possible. The experiment, therefore, went through without any general view of the whole situation being attained. Had such been possible, there can be no doubt at all that the war could have been shortened enough to keep the world back from the neighbourhood of spiritual and even material bankruptcy in which it finds itself to-day. The armed confrontation of the two types, while it has yielded a result that may well fill us with hope, took place at a moment of human evolution when it was bound to be immensely expensive. Material development had far exceeded social development, mankind, so to say, had become clever without becoming wise, and the war had to be fought as a purely destructive effort. Had it come at a later stage of evolution, so great a mobilization of social power as the war caused might have been taken advantage of to unify the nation to a completely coherent structure which the cessation of

the external stimulating pressure would have left
firmly and nobly established.

AFTER THE WAR.

The psychological situation left by the conclusion
of the war is likely to attract an increasing amount
of attention as time passes, and it may be of interest
to examine it in the light of the principles that
we have been making use of in dealing with the
war.

It is a fact fundamental in psychology that the
state of war furnishes the most powerful of all
stimuli to the social instinct. It sets in motion a tide
of common feeling by the power of which union
and energy of purpose and self-sacrifice for the
good of the social unit become possible to a degree
unknown under any other circumstances. The war
furnished many instances of the almost miraculous
efficacy of this stimulus. Perhaps the most effective
example of all, even by the side of the steely
fortitude of France and the adventurous despera-
tion of England, was the fact that the dying Austrian
Empire could be galvanized for four years into
aggressive gestures lifelike beyond simulation.

The effect of this great liberation of feeling was
to supersede the precarious equilibrium of society
by a state very much more stable. Before the war
moral power had come to the individual chiefly
from the lesser herds in which he took part, and
but little from the nation as a whole. Society had
the appearance of stability because the forces at
work were relatively small in proportion to the
inertia of the whole fabric. But the actual firmness
of the structure was small, and the individual led
a life emotionally thin and tame because the social
feelings were localized and faint. With the outbreak of war the national unit became the source
of moral power, social feeling became wide in its

basis and strong in intensity. To the individual
life became more intense and more significant, and
in essence, in spite of horror and pain, better worth
living ; the social fabric, moreover, displayed a
new stability and a capacity for resisting dis-
turbances that would have effectually upset its
equilibrium in time of peace. The art of government,
in fact, became actually easier to practise, though
it had a superficial appearance of being more
difficult from the comparative rapidity with which
the progress of events unmasked the quack.
Successful practitioners were, it will be remembered, always ready to call attention to the unprecedented difficulty of their labours, while shrewdly
enough profiting by the fact that in the actual
tasks of government—the creation of interest, the
development of unity and the nourishing of impulse
—their difficulties had wholly disappeared.

With the cessation of war this great stream of
moral power began rapidly to dry up at its source.
Thinly continuing to trickle for a time as it were
from habit, it is already almost dry. There is
doubtless a tendency among responsible personages
to persuade themselves that it still flows with all
the power that made the war a veritable golden
age of government. Such a persuasion is natural
and fully to be expected. It would be difficult
for those who have directed with whatever want of
skill a power so great to avoid coming in time
to be a little confused between the direction of
power and the production of it, and to think that
they still command the moral resources which war
gave so abundantly. Such a mistake is likely to
prove one of the elements of danger, though
perhaps only a minor one, in the present situation.

Western society, with perhaps even Western civilization, is in a situation of great interest to the
sociologist, and probably also of some considerable

danger. There are certain chief elements of
danger which we may attempt to define.

First, with the end of the war the mental orientation of the individual has undergone a great
change. National feeling is no longer able to supply
him with moral vigour and interest. He must
turn once more to his class for what the nation
as a whole has been so much more efficiently supply-
ing. Life has regained for him much of its old
tameness, the nation in which he has lived vividly
during the war is resuming its vagueness and
becoming once more merely the state, remote and
quasi-hostile. But the war has shown him what
interest and moral vigour are in life, and he will
not easily accept the absence of these ; he has
acquired the appetite for them, he has, so to speak,
tasted blood. The tasteless social dietary of pre-war
England is not likely to satisfy his invigorated
palate.

Secondly, the transition from war to peace is in
an imperfectly organized society a process necessarily dangerous because it involves the change from
a condition of relative moral stability to one of
relative moral instability. To get back to the
precise state of delicately balanced but essentially
insecure equilibrium of society before the war
would seem, in fact, already shown to be impossible.
The war ran its course without any attempt being
made to replace the system of class segregation,
through which the social instinct works in our
society, by any more satisfactory mechanism.
Before the war class segregation had reached a condition in which the individual had ceased to be
conscious of the national unit as possessing any
practical significance for himself, while his class
was the largest unit he was capable of recognizing as a source of moral power and an object
of effort. There was no class which as such and

in relation to other classes was capable of submitting to any restraint or self-sacrifice in the
interests of the nation as a whole. Of course,
in each case it was possible for a class by a
very easy process of rationalization to show that its
interests were those of the nation at large, but
this was merely the effect of the moral blindness
to which class segregation inevitably leads. Since
every one of us is classified somehow, it is not
easy to grasp how completely class segregation
obtains throughout our society, and how fully in
times of peace it replaces national unity. Those
occupying the lower social strata may be very fully
aware of the intensity of class feeling and how
complete a substitute for national feeling it affords
at the upper end of the social scale, just as those
in the upper strata may be very much alive to
the class bitterness of their inferiors ; but it is difficult for both to believe how complete are segregation and its consequences throughout the whole
social gamut.

It is to this state of society that the return from
the relative unity of war must be. The few conventional restraints upon the extremity of class
feeling that were in any kind of activity before
the war have been very greatly weakened. Change
has become familiar, violence has been glorified
in theory and shown to be effective in practice,
the prestige of age has been undermined, and the
sanctity of established things defied.

It would, indeed, seem that to re-establish a society
based solely on class segregation, and relying upon
the maintenance by it of a state of equilibrium, will
be a matter of some difficulty, and it will probably
be a mistake to depend altogether on fatigue, on
the relaxation of feeling, and on the celebration of
victory as stabilizing forces.

Thirdly, there is no reason to suppose that the

tendencies of society which made possible so huge
a disaster as the war have been in any, way corrected
by it. Great efforts are being made at present to
establish conditions which will prevent future wars.
Such efforts are entirely, admirable, but it is must
be remembered that after all war, is no more than
a symptom of social defects. If, therefore, war as
a symptom is merely, suppressed, valuable as that
will be in controlling the waste and destruction of
life and effort, indeed indispensable to, any kind
of vigorous mental life, it may leave untouched
potentialities of disaster comparable even with war
itself.

It was pointed out many years ago in the essays
incorporated in this book that human society tends
to restrict influence and leadership to minds of a
certain type, and that these minds tend to have
special and characteristic defects. Thus human
affairs are in general under the direction of a
class of thought that is not merely not the best
of which the mind is capable, but tends to certain
characteristic fallacies and to certain characteristic
kinds of blindness and incapacity. The class of
mind to which power in society, gravitates I have
ventured to describe as the stable type. Its characteristic virtues and deficiencies have been described
more than once in this book, and we need do no
more here than recall its vigour and resistiveness, its
accessibility to the voice of the herd and its resistiveness to and even horror of the new in feeling
and experience. The predominance of this type
has been rigorously maintained throughout the war.
This is why the war has been fought with a mere
modicum of help from the human intellect, and why
the result must be regarded as a triumph for the
common man rather than for the ruling classes.
The war was won by, the inflexible resolution of
the common citizen and the common soldier. No

country has shown itself to be directed by the higher powers of the intellect, and nowhere has the continued action of clear, temperate, vigorous, and comprehensive thought made itself manifest, because even the utmost urgency of warfare failed to dislodge the stable-minded type from its monopoly of prestige and power. What the necessities of war could not do there is certainly no magic in peace to bring about. Society, therefore, is setting out upon what is generally regarded as a new era of hope without the defect that made the war possible having in any degree been corrected. Certain supposedly immutable principles such as democracy and national self-determination are regarded by some as being mankind's guarantees against disaster. To the psychologist such principles represent mere vague and fluctuating drifts of feeling, arising out of deep instinctive needs, but not fully and powerfully embodying such ; as automatic safeguards of society, their claims are altogether bogus, and cannot be ranked as perceptibly higher than those of the ordinary run of political nostrums and doctrinaire specifics. Society can never be safe until the direction of it is entrusted only, to those who possess high capacity rigorously trained and acute sensitiveness to experience and to feeling.

Statecraft, after all, is a difficult art, and it seems unreasonable to leave the choice of those who practise it to accident, to heredity, or to the possession of the wholly irrelevant gifts that take the fancy of the crowd. The result of such methods of selection is not even a mere random choice from the whole population, but shows a steady drift towards the establishment in power of a type in certain ways almost characteristically, unfitted for the tasks of government. The fact that man has always shirked the heavy, intellectual and moral labour of founding a scientific and truly expert statecraft may contain a germ of hope for the future, in that it shows where effort may be usefully expended. But it cannot but justify uneasiness as to the immediate future of society. The essential factor in society is the subordination of the individual will to social needs. Our statecraft is still ignorant of how this can be made a fair and honest bargain to the individual and to the state, and recent events have convinced a very large proportion of mankind that accepted methods of establishing this social cohesion have proved to them at any rate the worst of bargains.

THE INSTABILITY OF CIVILIZATION.

The foregoing considerations are enough, perhaps, to make one wonder whether, after all, Western civilization may not be about to follow its unnumbered predecessors into decay and dissolution. There can be no doubt that such a suspicion is oppressing many thoughtful minds at the present time. It is not likely to be dispelled by the contemplation of history or by the nature of recent events. Indeed, the view can be maintained very plausibly that all civilizations must tend ultimately to break down, that they reach sooner or later a period when their original vigour is worn out, and then collapse through internal disruption or outside pressure. It is even believed by some that Western civilization already shows the evidences of decline which in its predecessors have been the forerunners of destruction. When we remember that our very short period of recorded history includes the dissolution of civilizations so elaborate as those of the Chaldeans, the Assyrians, the Egyptians, and of the Incas, that a social structure so complex as that but lately disclosed in Crete could leave no trace in human

16

memory but a faint and dubious whisper of tradition, and that the dawn of history finds civilization already old, we can scarcely resist the conclusion that social life has, more often than one can bear to contemplate, swung laboriously up to a meaningless apogee and then lapsed again into darkness. We know enough of man to be aware that each of these unnumbered upward movements must have been infinitely painful, must have been at least as fruitful of torture, oppression, and anguish as the ones of which we know the history, and yet each was no more than the swing of a pendulum and a mere fruitless oscillation landing man once more at his starting point, impoverished and broken, with perhaps more often than not no transmissible vestige of his greatness.

If we limit our view to the historical scale of time and the exclusively human outlook, we seem almost forced to accept the dreadful hypothesis that in the very structure and substance of all human constructive social efforts there is embodied a principle of death, that there is no progressive impulse but must become fatigued, that the intellect can provide no permanent defence against a vigorous barbarism, that social complexity is necessarily weaker than social simplicity, and that fineness of moral fibre must in the long run succumb to the primitive and coarse.

Let us consider, however, what comments may be made on this hypothesis in view of the biological conceptions of man which have been put forward in this book. At the same time an opportunity is afforded to put in a more continuous form the view of society that has necessarily been touched on so far in an interrupted and incidental way.

Whatever may be one's view as to the larger pretensions that are put forward as to the significance and destiny of man, there can be no doubt

that it is indispensable to recognize the full impli-
cations of his status as an animal completely
indigenous in the zoological series. The whole of
his physical and mental structure is congruous with
that of other living beings, and is constantly giving
evidence of the complicated network of relationships
by which he is bound to them.

The accumulation of knowledge is steadily ampli-
fying the range over which this congruity with the
natural order can be demonstrated, and is showing
more and more fully that practical understanding
and foresight of man's behaviour are attained in
proportion as this hypothesis of the complete
" naturalness " of man is adhered to.

The endowment of instinct that man possesses
is in every detail cognate with that of other animals,
provides no element that is not fully represented
elsewhere, and above all—however little the individual man may be inclined to admit it—is in no
degree less vigorous and intense or less important
in relation to feeling and activity than it is in related
animals. This supremely important side of mental
life, then, will be capable of continuous illustration
and illumination by biological methods. It is on
the intellectual side of mental life that man's congruity with other animals is least obvious at first
sight. The departure from type, however, is
probably a matter of degree only, and not of quality.
Put in the most general terms, the work of the intellect is to cause delay between stimulus and response,
and under circumstances to modify the direction of the latter. We may suppose all stimulation
to necessitate response, and that such response must
ultimately occur with undiminished total energy.
The intellect, however, is capable of delaying such
response, and within limits of directing its path
so that it may superficially show no relation to the
stimulus of which it is the discharge. If we extend

the word stimulation to include the impulses arising
from instinct, and grant that the delaying and
deflecting influence of the intellect may be indefinitely enlarged, we have an animal in which instinct
is as vigorous as in any of its primitive ancestors,
but which is superficially scarcely an instinctive
animal at all. Such is the case of man. His instinctive impulses are so greatly masked by the variety
of response that his intellect opens to him that he
has been commonly regarded until quite recent
times as a practically non-instinctive creature,
capable of determining by reason his conduct and
even his desires. Such a conception made it almost
impossible to gain any help in human psychology,
from the study of other animals, and scarcely less
difficult to evolve a psychology which would be
of the least use in foreseeing and controlling the
behaviour of man.

No understanding of the causes of stability and
instability in human society is possible until the
undiminished vigour of instinct in man is fully,
recognized.

The significance of this rich instinctive endowment lies in the fact that mental health depends
upon instinct finding a balanced but vigorous expression in functional activity. The response to instinct
may be infinitely varied, and may even, under
certain circumstances, be not more than symbolic
without harm to the individual as a social unit, but
there are limits beyond which the restriction of
it to indirect and symbolic modes of expression
cannot be carried without serious effects on
personality. The individual in whom direct instinctive expression is unduly limited acquires a spiritual
meagreness which makes him the worst possible
social material.

All recorded history shows that society developing under the conditions that have obtained up

to the present time—developing, that is to say,
spontaneously under the random influences of an
uncontrolled environment of the individual—does not
permit to the average man that balanced instinctive
expression which is indispensable for the formation
of a rich, vigorous, and functionally active personality. It has been one of my chief efforts in this
book to show that the social instinct, while in itself
the very foundation of society, takes, when its action
is undirected and uncontrolled, a principal part in
restricting the completeness and efficacy of the social
impulse. This instinct is doubly responsible for
the defects which have always inhered in society
through the personal impoverishment of its individual constituents. In the first place, it is the
great agent by which the egoistic instincts are
driven into dwarfed, distorted, and symbolic modes
of expression without any regard for the objective
social necessity of such oppressive regulation. In
the second place, it is an instinct which, while it
embodies one of the deepest and potentially most
invigorating passions of the soul, tends automatically
to fall out of vigorous and constant activity with
the expansion of societies. It is the common
character of large societies to suffer heavily from
the restrictive effect on personality of the social
instinct, and at the same time to suffer in the highest
degree from the debilitation of the common social
impulse. Only in the smallest groups, such as
perhaps was early republican Rome, can the common
impulse inform and invigorate the whole society.
As the group expands and ceases to feel the constant
pressure of an environment it no longer has to
fear, the common impulse droops, and the society
becomes segregated into classes, each of which
a lesser herd within the main body and under the
reciprocated pressure of its fellows, now yields to
its members the social feeling which the main body

can no longer provide. The passage of the small, vigorous, homogeneous and fiercely patriotic group into the large, lax, segregated and ultimately decadent group is a commonplace of history. In highly segregated peoples the restrictive effect of the social instinct upon personality has usually been to some extent relaxed, and a relatively rich personal development has been possible. Such an amplification has always, however, been limited to privileged classes, has always been accompanied by a weakening of the national bond, and a tendency of the privileged class to the sincere conviction that its interests are identical with those of the nation. No nation has ever succeeded in liberating the personality of its citizens from the restrictive action of the social instinct and at the same time in maintaining national homogeneity, and common impulse. In a small community, intercommunication among its individual members is free enough to keep common feeling intense and vigorous. As the community increases in size the general intercommunication becomes attenuated, and with this common feeling is correspondingly weakened. If there were no other mechanism capable of inducing common action than the faint social stimulus coming from the nation at large, a segregated society would be incapable of national enterprise. There is, however, another mechanism which we may call leadership, using the word in a certain special sense. All social groups are more or less capable of being led, and it is manifest that the leadership of individuals, or perhaps more usually of classes, has been a dominant influence in the expansion and enterprise of all civilizations of which we have any knowledge. It is only in the small communities that we can detect evidence of a true common impulse shared alike by all the members acting as the cause of expansion. In larger groups, auto-

cracies and dynasties, Pharaohs and Nebuchad-
nezzars have imposed the impulse of expansion upon
the people, and by virtue of human susceptibility
to leadership have secured a virtual, though only a
secondary, common purpose.

Now leadership, potent as it undoubtedly is in
calling forth the energy of the social instinct, is
essentially a limited and therefore an exhaustible
force. It depends for continued vigour upon
successful enterprise. While it is succeeding there
are only wide limits to the moral power it can
set free and command, but in the face of misfortune
and disaster its limitations become obvious, and its
power inevitably declines. On the other hand, the
moral power yielded by a true community of
feeling, and not imposed by leadership, is enormously
more resistant and even indestructible by failure
and defeat. History gives many examples of the
encounters of communities of these two types—the
led society and the homogeneous society—and in
spite of the invariably greater size and physical
power of the former, frequently records the astound-
ingly successful resistance its greater moral vigour
has given to the latter. This is perhaps why
Carthage beat in vain against little Rome, and
certainly why Austria failed to subdue Switzer-
land.

All large societies that have had their day and
have fallen from their zenith by internal dissolution
or outward attack have been given their impulse
to expansion by leadership and have depended on
it for their moral power. If society is to continue
to depend for its enterprise and expansion upon
leadership, and can find no more satisfactory source
of moral power, it is, to say the least, highly
probable that civilizations will continue to rise and
fall in a dreadful sameness of alternating aspiration
and despair until perhaps some lucky accident of

confusion finds for humanity in extinction the rest it could never win for itself in life.

There is, however, reason to suppose that susceptibility to leadership is a characteristic of relatively primitive social types, and tends to diminish with increasing social complexity. I have already called attention to and attempted to define the apparently specific psychological differences between Germany and England before and during the war. These differences I attributed to variations in the type of reaction to herd instinct shown by the two peoples. The aggressive social type represented by Germany and analogous with that characteristic of the predaceous social animals I regarded as being relatively primitive and simple. The socialized type represented by England and presenting analogies with that characteristic of many social insects I regarded as being, though imperfect as are all the human examples available for study up to the present time, more complex and less primitive, and representing at any rate a tendency towards a satisfactory solution of the problems with which man as a gregarious animal is surrounded. Now, it is a very obvious fact that the susceptibility to leadership shown by Germany and by England before the war was remarkably different. The common citizen of Germany was strikingly open to and dependent upon discipline and leadership, and seemed to have a positive satisfaction in leaving to his masters the management of his social problems and accepting with alacrity the solutions that were imposed upon him. The nation consequently presented a close knit uniformity of purpose, a singleness of national consciousness and effort that gave it an aspect of moral power of the most formidable kind. In England a very different state of affairs prevailed. The common citizen was apt to meet with indifference or resentment all efforts to change the social

structure, and it had long been a political axiom
that "reform" should always await an irresistible
demand for it.   Instances will be within every one's
memory of politicians who met with crushing rebuffs
through regarding the supposed desirability of a
reform as a justification for imposing it.   This
almost sullen indifference to great projects and
ideals, this unwillingness to take thought in the
interests of the nation and the empire in spite of
the apostolic zeal of the most eloquent political
prophets, was generally regarded as evidence of
a weakness and slackness in the body politic that
could not but threaten disaster.   And yet in the
trials of the war the moral stability of England
showed itself to be superior to that of Germany,
which, in those rough waters, it jostled as mercilessly
and as effectually as did the brass pot the earthen
crock in the fable.

During the war itself the submission to leadership
that England showed was characteristic of the
socialized type.   It was to a great extent spontaneous, voluntary, and undisciplined, and gave
repeated evidence that the passage of inspiration
was essentially from the common people to its
leaders rather than from the leaders to the common
people.   When the current of inspiration sets persistently in this direction, as it unquestionably did in
England, it is very plain that the primitive type
of leadership that has led so many civilizations
to disaster is no longer in unmodified action.

Germany has provided the most complete example
of a culture of leadership that has ever been
recorded, and has gone through the phases of her
evolution with a precision which should make her
case an illustration classical for all history.   With
a people showing strongly the characteristics of the
aggressive social type, and a social structure deeply
and rigidly segregated, the nation was ideally

susceptible to discipline and leadership, and a leading class was available which possessed an almost superhuman prestige. The opportunity given to leadership was exploited with great energy and thoroughness and with an intelligence that by its intensity almost made up for being nowhere really profound. With all these advantages and the full uses of the huge resources science has made available to intelligently concerted effort, an extremely formidable power was created. The peoples of the socialized type towards whom from the first its hostility was scarcely veiled were under obvious disadvantages in rivalry with it. Their social type made it impossible for them to combine and organize themselves against what was to them no more than a vaguely hypothetical danger. Against peaceful conquest by Germany in the industrial sphere England was therefore practically helpless, and to it would probably in time have succumbed. Paradox as it may seem, there can be no doubt that it was in war only that England could contend with Germany on equal terms. Paradoxically again, it was war for which England was reluctant and Germany was eager.

War brought Germany into contact with the, to her, inexplicable ferocity of peoples of the socialized type under attack, and it was by this disappointment that the first blow to her morale was struck. The wastage of modern warfare must very soon have begun to impair the isolation and prestige of the officer class through increasingly free importation from without the pale. With this necessarily began to be sapped the absolute and rigid segregation on which leadership of the type we are considering so largely depends. At the same time, the general tendency of the increasing pressure of war is to wear down class segregation over the whole social field. This tendency, which intensified and invigorated the morale of her enemies would work steadily against the leadership morale of Germany. These factors must no doubt be added to the moral need for aggression, the exhaustion consequent upon forced offensives, and the specific intolerance of failure and retreat that combined to bring down the strongest example of the predaceous led society that history records.

Some Characters of a Rational Statecraft.

If the foregoing discussion has been sound, we may attribute the impermanence of all civilizations of which we have knowledge to the failure of society to preserve with increasing magnitude of its communities a true homogeneity, and a progressive integration of its elements. We have seen that there is a type of society—distinguished here as the socialized type—in which a trace of this integrative tendency can be detected at work. Under the threat of war this tendency is accelerated in its action, and can attain a moderate, though very far indeed from a complete, degree of development. In the absence of such a powerful stimulus to homogeneity, however, segregation reasserts itself, and the society, necessarily deprived by its type of the advantages of leadership, becomes confused, disunited, and threatened with disruption. It seems probable, indeed, that the integrative tendency unaided and uncontrolled is too weak to surmount the obstacles with which it has to contend, and to anticipate disruption by welding the elements of society into a common life and common purpose. It has already been repeatedly suggested that these difficulties, due as they are to the human power of various reaction, can be met only by the interposition of the intellect as an active factor in the problem of the direction of society. In other words, the progressive evolution of society has reached a point where the construction and use of a scientific statecraft will become an indispensable factor in further development and the only means of arresting the dreary oscillations between progress and relapse which have been so ominous a feature in human history. We are perhaps in a position to-day to suggest tentatively some of the principles on which such a statecraft might be built.

It would have to, be based on a full recognition of the biological status of man, and to work out the tendencies which as an animal he is pursuing and must pursue. If we have evidence of the only course evolution can follow satisfactorily, then it is clear that any social and legislative effort not in line with that course must be entirely wasted. Moreover, since we are proceeding on the hypothesis that direct conscious effort is now a necessary factor in the process, we must clear our minds of the optimistic determinism which regards man as a special pet of nature and the pessimistic determinism which would reduce him to a mere spectator of his destiny. The trained and conscious mind must come to be regarded as a definite factor in man's environment, capable of occupying there a larger and larger area.

Such a statecraft would recognize how fully man is an instinctive being and how his mental vigour and stability depend entirely upon instinctive expression being adequate. The tyrannous power of the social instinct in repressing and distorting instinctive expression would have to be controlled and directed with the purpose of enlarging the personal and social effectiveness of the individual to the maximum extent ; the social instinct would no longer be left to operate on the individual under the random direction of custom and habit, of fashion and social whim, or for the satisfaction of the jealousy of age.

Perhaps most important of all, a scientific state-craft would understand that the social instinct itself is as deep and powerful as any, and hungrily demands intense and positive gratification and expression. The social instinct drives the individual to seek union with some community of his fellows. The whole national body is in the present state of society the smallest unit in which the individual can find complete and permanent satisfaction. As long as the average man's sense of possession in the state is kept so low as it is at present, as long as the sense of moral inequality between himself and his fellows is so vigorously maintained, so long will he continue to make his class rather than his nation the object of social passion, and so long will society continue to breed within itself a principle of death.

The exploration of the psychology of man's social relations has been left almost exclusively to the operation of what we may call the method of prophetic intuition, and there is no branch of knowledge where the fumbling methods of unclarified intuition have introduced more confusion. Intuitions in the sphere of feeling—moral intuitions—have more than the usual tendency of intuitions to appear as half-truths surrounded and corrupted by fantasies of the seer and isolated from correlation with the rest of knowledge. Let us consider, for example, the intuitional doctrine of philosophic anarchism. The nucleus of truth in this is the series of perfectly sound psychological conceptions that all social discipline should be, as experienced by the individual, spontaneous and voluntary, that man possesses the instinctive endowment which renders possible a voluntary organization of society, and that in such a society order would be more effectively maintained than under our present partially compulsory system. This nucleus, which of course is not understood or expressed in these definite psychological terms by the anarchist, is apt to be associated with dogmas which altogether obscure its strictly unassailable truth. Communism, again, is another doctrine which contains its core of psychological truth, namely, that individual property is an economic convention rather than a psychological necessity, and that social inequality is an infirmity of the state rather than its foundation stone. As it is exemplified in practice, however, communism is so deeply tainted by the belief in an inverted class segregation of its own, and by a horror of knowledge, that its elements of reality are wholly obscured and rendered useless.

Every doctrine that makes disciples freely must contain in it some embodiment of psychological reality, however exiguous ; but where it has been arrived at by the methods of the prophet, there is no reason to expect that stress will be laid on the true more than on the false elements of the doctrinal scheme, and experience shows that the inessential falsity has for the expositor as many, if not more, attractions than the essential truth. An expert statecraft would be able to identify the real elements of discovery that were present in any fresh prophetic appeal to public belief, and would be able at any rate to save the state from the condition of petrified embarrassment into which it now falls when faced by social dogmas and experiments which win attention and adhesion while at the same time they outrage convention and common sense.

The examination of the functional satisfactoriness of society, which has been a chief object of this book, has yielded a certain general body of con-clusions. An attempt will now be made to summarize these in a compact and even dogmatic form, and to add what further element of definition seems indispensable for clearness.

1. All societies of which we have any, knowledge have shown two general defects—they have proved unable to develop and direct more than a small fraction of the resources they, theoretically possess, and they have been impermanent, so that time after time laborious accumulations of constructive effort have been wasted. According to our analysis these defects are due to the drift of power into the hands of the stable-minded class, and to the derivation of moral power and enterprise from the mechanisms of leadership and class segregation.

2. A society, in order to have stability and full functional effectiveness, must be capable of a continually progressive absorption of its individual members into the general body—an uninterrupted movement towards a complete moral homogeneity.

3. A tendency towards a progressive integration of this kind can be detected in society to-day by direct observation. It is weak and its effects are fluctuating, so that there is doubt whether it can, unless directly encouraged by human effort, counteract the forces which up till now have always limited social evolution to movements of oscillation rather than of true progress.

4. The only way in which society can be made safe from disruption or decay is by the intervention of the conscious and instructed intellect as a factor among the forces ruling its development.

This last doctrine has been repeatedly stated, but we have perhaps scarcely defined it precisely enough to avoid misunderstanding. Some such definition is our concluding task. Of all the elements we find in a general examination of the whole biological series the human intellect is the one that most clearly gives the impression of a new and intrusive factor. The instinctive side of man, with its derivatives, such as his morals, his altruism, and his aspirations, falls very easily into line with the rest of the natural order, and is seen to be at work in modes which nowhere show any essential new departure. The intellect, however, brings with it a capacity for purpose as distinct from and additional to desire, and this does apparently introduce a factor virtually new to the biological series. The part that the purposive foresight of the intellect has been allowed to take in human affairs has always been limited by instinctive inhibitions. This limitation has effectually prevented man from defining his situation in the world, and he remains a captive in the house of circumstance, restrained as effectually by the mere painted canvas of habit, convention, and fear as by the solid masonry of essential instinctive needs. Being denied the freedom, which is its indispensable source of vigour, the intellect has necessarily failed to get a clear, comprehensive, and temperate view of man's status and prospects, and has, of course, shrunk from the yet more exacting task of making itself responsible for his destiny. Nowhere has been and is the domination of the herd more absolute than in the field of speculation concerning man's general position and fate, and in consequence prodigies of genius have been expended in obscuring the simple truth that there is no responsibility for man's destiny anywhere at all outside his own responsibility, and that there is no remedy for his ills outside his own efforts. Western civilization has recently lost ten millions of its best lives as a result of the exclusion of the intellect from the general direction of society. So terrific an object lesson has made it plain enough how easy it is for man, all undirected and unwarned as he is, to sink to the irresponsible destructiveness of the monkey.

Such ostensible direction as societies obtain derives its sanction from one or more of three sources—the hereditary, the representative, and the official. No direction can be effective in the way needed for the preservation of society unless it comes from minds broad in outlook, deep in sympathy, sensitive to the new and strange in experience, capable of resisting habit, convention, and the other sterilizing influences of the herd, deeply learned in the human mind and vividly aware of the world. › Plainly enough, neither of the classes enumerated above is any more likely to possess these characteristics than any one else. To the representative and official classes there even attaches, at any rate theoretically, the suspicion that the methods by which they are chosen and promoted, while they obviously in no way favour fitness, may actually tend to favour unfitness. Of the hereditary class it may at any rate be said that while it does not in any special degree include the fit, its composition is random and in no way tainted by popular standards of suitability or by the prejudices and conventions of the examination room. It would seem, then, that none of the methods by which society appoints its directors shows any promise of working towards the effective intervention of the intellect in social affairs. In reaching this conclusion we have perhaps passed too lightly over the claims of the trained official as a possible nucleus of an ultimate scientific statecraft. The present-day controversies as to the nationalization of various industries give an especial interest to this very problem, and illustrate how unpromising a source of knowledge is political discussion. One group of advocates points to the obvious economies of conducting industry on the great scale and without the destructive effects of competition ; the other group points to the infirmities which always have infected officially conducted enterprises. Both sides would seem to be perfectly right so far and both to be wrong when

the first goes on to affirm that governments as they
now are can and do conduct industrial affairs quite
satisfactorily, and the second goes on to affirm that
the only mechanism by which society can get its
work effectively done is commercial competition, and
that the only adequate motive is greed. It seems
to have escaped the notice of both parties to the
controversy that no civilized country has evolved,
or begun to evolve, or thought of evolving a method
of selecting and training its public servants that
bears any rational relation to their fitness for the
art of government. It is not here denied that selection and training are both of them severe in many
countries. Mere severity, however, as long as it
is quite without relevance, is manifestly worthless.
We are forced to the conclusion, therefore, that to
expect an effective statecraft to be evolved from
the official, whether of the Chinese, the Prussian,
or any other type, is a mere dream. To encourage
such a hope would be to strengthen the grip of
the unsatisfactory stable-minded class upon the gullet
of society. The evidence then shows that among
the mechanisms whereby the directors of society
are chosen there is none that favours that intervention of the conscious and instructed intellect that we
have suggested is necessary to the effective evolution of civilization. Nowhere in the structure of
society is there a class tending to develop towards
this goal. Since from the point of view of social
effectiveness segregation into classes has been
entirely random, the appearance of such a
class would have been indeed an extraordinary
accident. Good as are the grounds for hoping that
human society may ultimately mature into a coherent
structure possessed of comprehensive and intelligent
direction, it would be no more than idle optimism
to suppose that there is any institution or class now
existing which promises to inspire a fundamental

reconstruction. If the effective intrusion of the intellect into social affairs does happily occur, it will come from no organ of society now recognizable, but through a slow elevation of the general standard of consciousness up to the level at which will be possible a kind of freemasonry and syndicalism of the intellect. Under such circumstances free communication through class barriers would be possible, and an orientation of feeling quite independent of the current social segregation would become manifest.

Throughout the enormously, long period during which modern man has been established on the earth human society has, been left to the uncontrolled contention of constructive and destructive forces, and in the long run the destructive have always proved the stronger. Whether the general level of consciousness will reach the height necessary to give a decisive predominance to constructive tendencies, and whether such a development will occur in time to save Western civilization from the fate of its predecessors, are open questions. The small segment of the social process of which we have direct knowledge in the events of the day has no very encouraging appearance. Segregation has reasserted itself effectively ; the dominion of the stable and resistive mind is as firmly established as ever, and no less dull and dangerous ; while it is plain how far, in the atmosphere of relaxation and fatigue, the social inspiration of the common man has sunk from the high constancy of spirit by which throughout the long pilgrimage of war so many weary feet have been upborne, so many dry lips refreshed.

INDEX

COSIMO is an innovative publisher of books and publications that inspire, inform and engage readers worldwide. Our titles are drawn from a range of subjects including health, business, philosophy, history, science and sacred texts. We specialize in using print-on-demand technology (POD), making it possible to publish books for both general and specialized audiences and to keep books in print indefinitely. With POD technology new titles can reach their audiences faster and more efficiently than with traditional publishing.

> **Permanent Availability:** Our books & publications never go out-of-print.

> **Global Availability:** Our books are always available online at popular retailers and can be ordered from your favorite local bookstore.

COSIMO CLASSICS brings to life unique, rare, out-of-print classics representing subjects as diverse as *Alternative Health, Business and Economics, Eastern Philosophy, Personal Growth, Mythology, Philosophy, Sacred Texts, Science, Spirituality* and much more!

COSIMO-on-DEMAND publishes your books, publications and reports. If you are an Author, part of an Organization, or a Benefactor with a publishing project and would like to bring books back into print, publish new books fast and effectively, would like your publications, books, training guides, and conference reports to be made available to your members and wider audiences around the world, we can assist you with your publishing needs.

Visit our website at www.cosimobooks.com to learn more about Cosimo, browse our catalog, take part in surveys or campaigns, and sign-up for our newsletter.

And if you wish please drop us a line at info@cosimobooks.com. We look forward to hearing from you.

Printed in the United States
87687LV00001B/38/A

9 781596 050761